Bitter, Bitter Tears

Nineteenth-Century Diarists and Twentieth-Century Grief Theories

The University of Minnesota Press
gratefully acknowledges the assistance for publication
provided by David and Sherrill Fesler.

Bitter, Bitter Tears

Nineteenth-Century Diarists and Twentieth-Century Grief Theories

Paul C. Rosenblatt

University of Minnesota Press • Minneapolis

Copyright © 1983 by the University of Minnesota.
All rights reserved.
Published by the University of Minnesota Press,
2037 University Avenue Southeast, Minneapolis, MN 55414
Printed in the United States of America.

Library of Congress Cataloging in Publication Data

Rosenblatt, Paul C.
    Bitter, bitter tears.

    Bibliography: p.
    Includes index.
    1. Grief. 2. Diaries—History and criticism.
I. Title.
BF575.G7R67 1983   155.9'37   83-3485
ISBN 0-8166-1244-7
ISBN 0-8166-1247-1 (pbk.)

". . . came to steamer. All the folks came down. It was killing work for me to say farewell. This done & I must not look mournfully into the past. We are not out of sight of land. . . . I only cried as the steamer sailed away—bitter, bitter tears."

Diary of Nellie Wetherbee, unpublished manuscript, Bancroft Library, University of California, Berkeley, entry of March 5, 1860.

***

"My darling only brother is dead. . . . It was only a short letter Selina wrote with her heart bleeding, almost breaking. . . . I cannot wish the dear one back. His body lies beside dear Susan's now. I hope his soul is with hers in heaven. . . . The bitter tears will come. I cannot keep them back."

Diary of Mrs. Charles C. Carpenter (Feronica Nancy Rice Carpenter), unpublished manuscript on microfilm at Public Archives of Canada, Ottawa, entry of June 12, 1863.

Preface

In 1967 I came across the diary of Mollie Dorsey Sanford (1959) and was fascinated by it. At that time I was doing scholarly work on romantic love, and the Sanford diary was so rich that I was persuaded that diaries could be a valuable source of information on love and many other aspects of people's closest relationships. During the early and middle 1970s I tracked down the published diaries I could find at various local libraries, with the intent of developing a bibliography and a set of research notes on those diaries that dealt with any aspect of close relationships. Unfortunately, many of the published diaries seemed to have been edited, and it was almost impossible to determine what had been removed through editing.

When an opportunity for a sabbatical year with freedom to do research arose (the 1977-1978 school year), I decided to spend a substantial amount of it tracking down unpublished nineteenth-century diaries with material on close relationships. At that time I still had not decided to write about grief, though I had been doing research on grief and thought I had a strong base from which to study it. My first visits to archives made it clear that grief was the most common aspect of close relationships that was represented in the diaries. A few diaries dealt with marital disenchantment, a few with courtship, a few with problems of childrearing; but many dealt with deaths and separations.

Work in the archives was demanding. It was physically exhausting to spend long hours reading difficult handwriting, breathing the inevitable dust of stored and deteriorating paper. In addition, the diaries that gripped me strongly, that gave me a strong sense of the personality and concerns of the diarist, were often painful to read. The most self-disclosing diaries, diaries by people I came to feel that I knew relatively well, gave poignant and often painfully detailed accounts of personal and family tragedies. On my early visits to archives, I would return to my motel or hotel room after an archive closed for the evening emotionally and physically exhausted, too drained to do anything but sleep.

The work with the diaries was also rewarding. I was learning about people from the diaries, learning in a social-science sense and also in a personal-awareness sense. For me the process of getting to know people long dead, especially people who had never been mentioned in history textbooks, was something like looking into a spiritual abyss. Perhaps it was simply that reading page after page of the private records and reflections of someone known to few or no living people was a confrontation with mortality and the meaning of life. The contrast between the vitality and immediacy of the diaries and the obscurity of the diarists was sobering. If that were not enough to make issues of mortality and the meaning of life salient, these issues were addressed directly in many of the diaries.

The search for diaries with material on relationships was an adventure. The standard guides to manuscript collections rarely gave information about the aspects of relationships that a specific diary might deal with. Even the "finding aids" at the various archives were likely to be uninformative in that regard. So the feelings of discovery and excitement I experienced when I found rich diaries such as the Brisbane diaries, the Huntington diary, or the Snow diary were intense.

Nonetheless, my physical and emotional fatigue during my early trips to archives was a problem for me. I decided to fight the fatigue in two ways, by making some trips with my children and by visiting archives near people who would be good for me to visit at the end of a day's work. Thus, my son Seth Rosenblatt accompanied me on an expedition to the Wisconsin Historical Society, and my son Ira Rosenblatt came with me on an expedition to three archives in Iowa. Most of the archives I visited were near relatives, friends, or colleagues, and I am indebted to many people who provided the warm human contact that helped me to remain resilient despite the physically demanding and emotionally draining work in the archives. For support during my work in Chicago, I am indebted to many people, particularly to Rose and Harry Rosenblatt, and to Doris and Kurt Kopstein. In Toronto I benefited from contact with Janet Salaff, Ken and Karen Dion, and Fred and Pearl Katz and their children, Michael, Dvora, and Jenny. In Ottawa, I was sustained in part by the kindnesses of Robert Wake and his colleagues at Carleton University. My visit to New Haven was made more agreeable by the hospitality of Elaine Blechman-Beck and Arthur Beck, and my visit to Columbus, Ohio, benefited greatly from the hospitality of Joe Spitzner, Marian Cohn, and Jeff Spitzner. Finally, my work with archives in Southern California benefited from the hospitality of Joe and Jinks Albaum and of Harry, Lila, and Peter Weintraub.

Traveling to archives and surviving the reduced income of a sabbatical year was made easier by support from the University of Minnesota Agricultural Experiment Station. I am indebted to Keith Huston, who was director of the Experiment Station at the time I began wandering among archives, for his support of this and other projects. The Experiment Station also financed computer work with the diary material and typing of this manuscript. I am indebted to Sandra L. Titus, Roxanne M. Anderson, and Patricia A. Johnson for help with computing, and to Nancy Disch, Jane Schwanke, and Gloria Lawrence for fast and accurate typing through innumerable drafts of the manuscript.

Many, many people made comments on drafts of specific chapters or simply helped me to think through issues that I was wrestling with. The list of people I owe thanks to includes Sandra L. Titus, Cynthia Englund, Michael R. Cunningham, Alletta J. Hudgens, Anne M. Nevaldine, M. Geraldine Gage, David Klein, Janet W. Salaff, Sara Evans, Seth Rosenblatt, Richard A. Meckel, Reed Larson, Roxanne Marie Anderson, Jeffrey Lerner, Michael Baizerman, Patricia Johnson, Robert M. Coppinger, and Richard M. Abel, who as a senior editor for the University of Minnesota Press has helped immensely to move this project into book form.

As anyone who has worked with manuscript collections or has hunted rare books can testify, research like mine cannot be done without the help of many competent archivists, librarians, pages, and other archive and library staff members. To them also I am grateful.

Contents

Bitter, Bitter Tears

*Nineteenth-Century Diarists
and Twentieth-Century
Grief Theories*

1

Studying Grief in Diaries

This book examines grief over death and separation in 56 nine-teenth-century U.S. and Canadian diaries. Grief is defined here as the emotional reactions (including sorrow, anger, and depression) and the cognitive reactions (including confusion and obsessive review) to a loss.

There are risks in analyzing any aspect of human social life. Being analytic may deprive one of the comfort and satisfaction that are gained by ignoring, glossing over, and forgetting, or it may deprive one of emotional spontaneity. Satisfying curiosity about other people's relationships and losses may lead one to be preoccupied with thoughts of oneself and one's actual and potential losses, all of which may keep one from doing things that should be done and make one less useful or interesting to others. Thinking about losses can also be quite depressing. Yet reading a social-science study of relationship-endings may help some people to live with (or to learn how to live without) extreme or prolonged distress, depression, and sorrow.

It may help some people to know that in the diaries on which this book is based, grief bubbles up recurrently, that experiencing pangs of grief years after a loss is common among bereaved people. It may help to know that it is not unusual to experience a sense of the presence of someone who has died or moved far away. It may be useful to learn about emotional control in grief, about the impact of a loss on interactions among the people left behind, or about the effect of home care for a terminally ill relative. The material in this book can illuminate the reader's life and the lives of the people he or she knows.

To scholars who specialize in the study of grief and to the general reader this book offers, partly in the form of an expansion and clarification of the theory of grief work, a comprehensive view of the grief process. This view is sustained by quantitative analyses of the diary material and by excerpted quotes from the material. Among the important developments generated from the diary material are a sense of when people think about a loss and feel grief, strong evidence that grief for the losses of important people in one's life recurs frequently and may never be completely finished, and an analysis of the complexity involved in the anticipatory grief process.

The comparison of grief for deaths with grief for separations reveals some surprising long-term differences, though these differences can be easily understood in the perspective of the theory of grief work. A comparison of two categories of people experiencing loss as a result of separation—leavers and people who were left—provides additional perspective on the grief process, as do analyses involving the effects on grief of relationship closeness, coresidence with the lost before the loss, and duration of relationship.

The investigation of emotional control, as reported by the diarists, provides a strong sense of the normality of control in grief, of the value of control, and of the reasons why control might typically have no pathological outcome. The analysis of family phenomena in the grief process helps to clarify a number of commonly occurring aspects of the process. Family systems theory, attachment theory, symbolic interaction theory, family development theory, and reminder theory are used in probing the diary material and, in turn, are examined in the light of this material.

Throughout the book historical issues are dealt with. Work with the diary material provides perspective on the history of grief and related matters in the nineteenth century. Moreover, the apparent value of the diary material in illuminating grief and in helping to expand and clarify modern grief theories makes it imperative that the historical context of the diaries be continually kept in mind as a possible limitation to their usefulness.

Why Study Grief in Diaries?

The dictionary definition of the term *diary* is "a daily record of personal experiences and observations." But relatively few records of personal experiences and observations contain entries for every day. A definition that comes closer to encompassing the 56 personal documents labeled *diaries* in the present study is Fothergill's definition (1974, p. 3): "A diary is what a person writes when he says, 'I am writing my diary.'" Some of the diarists in the sample discussed in this book called their personal records "journals"; others called them "day books"; still others called them nothing at all. In the study reported in this book, a written document was considered to be a diary when a person called it a diary, journal, or daybook, or when it contained records of personal experiences or observations dated at least a few times per year.

Diaries have especially great promise in the study of loss. In contrast to most research materials, they can give a relatively fine texture to the records of reactions to loss, finer certainly than any retrospective account or any measurement made at one point in time. This texture allows one to see more clearly day-to-day changes, long-term trends, and the effects of specific events. Diaries can provide not only more detail, but more accuracy, as well as reactions less distorted by subsequent experiences and thought. Diaries can give greater accuracy for dates, people, places, and events than interview accounts or oral history material, because the diarist is usually recalling events that are fresh. The accuracy of a diary account may also be relatively great because a diary can provide a less censored report of reactions, a record of feelings and events that would in retrospective accounts be considered too trivial or too embarrassing to mention, if they were even recalled.

Diaries provide a record uncontaminated by a framework imposed by the researcher. In research involving interaction between researcher and person studied the researcher focuses, often in a very compelling way, the attention of the person studied. Some things are of interest to the researcher; others are not. Focus allows for an economic use of time and comparable data across respondents, but it means that much may be missed. Use of diarist-generated rather than researcher-generated data means that the primary information is not contaminated by the researcher's frameworks and questions.

To ask a question about guilt, for example, may create guilt in some people and guilt denial in others. The question may lead people to face issues about which they might feel guilt that they had not faced before, to be defensive about their guilt or lack of it, or to respond to the social pressure that questions about guilt might engender by persuading themselves that they have or have not felt guilt. Respondent-generated documents lack this kind of contamination from the researcher's questions. Moreover, use of nineteenth-century diaries means that the diaries have not been influenced by the theory of grief work (see chapter 3 for an outline of the theory), by any offshoots of it, or by other twentieth-century grief theories. The diarists have not been defining themselves or seeing themselves and their social world in the perspective of the twentieth-century theories explored in this volume.

With each diarist writing from a different perspective, research documentation is of necessity more anecdotal. In addition, the failure of a diarist to mention something is hard to interpret. Did the diarist who failed to mention spiritist beliefs or a sense of the presence of a deceased relative have no thoughts or experiences in these areas, or did these matters simply seem inappropriate to address in the diary? The lack of a researcher-imposed framework makes research more difficult in these regards, but it becomes easier to identify phenomena that current psychological, psychiatric, and social-science theories have overlooked. There are, in fact, many discussions in this book that go into theoretical areas that have not been in fashion. For example, the diary material leads to discussion of spiritist communication with the deceased, relationships with God from a family-systems perspective, and personal strategies for emotional self-control.

The privacy of a diary may permit the disclosure of thoughts and actions the diarist would be unlikely to disclose even to the most skilled interviewer—for example, thoughts disrespectful of a relative, thoughts of suicide, apparent hallucinations, rage at God, questioning of the existence or good will of God, and concern about one's own possible contribution to the death of a loved one. Of course people may deceive themselves, and may fail to mention in their diaries some crucial thoughts and events. But as one means of probing actions and thoughts that people are unlikely to own up to, the study of diaries certainly has promise.

Diaries provide rich, vital documentation—people propelled by their own concerns and emotions, writing in their own words, without prompting by someone else. Although vivid documentation adds, by contemporary epistemological standards, no weight to assertions, such documentation does help to communicate theoretical ideas more forcefully, more memorably, and more clearly to the reader (Rosenblatt, 1981). Although contemporary epistemology attaches no value to better understanding for more people, that may be a blind spot, arising perhaps in part from the fact that scholars with epistemological interests have great verbal ability and value the assimilation of abstruse knowledge. Yet there may be little in the social sciences or psychology that most readers could not understand if it were communicated well. Vivid documentation such as that provided by diary materials can aid in that communication.

In addition, if one believes that scholarly theories are inseparable from documentation (Kuhn, 1962), that the whole package of theory, methods, and classic research studies is learned and is also used in investigation, the extension of familiar scholarly ideas into new arenas of data opens up those ideas to change. Even if this book adds no entirely new idea to the theory of grief work, to family-systems theory, or to other theories, the provision of documentation and illustrations from diary material has the potential to change the way those theories are eventually understood and used. Rich diary material may provide less support for the selective vision that is both beneficial and harmful when one works within a given theory. Vivid documentation, such as diary material, when used in conjunction with a theoretical framework, may inevitably lead to regions that have been ignored.

The Sample

This book deals only with diary entries written in the nineteenth century, written predominantly in North America, and in English or English translation. These limits arose first of all from a need to put some boundaries on the investigation—boundaries to keep the study manageable and to limit the range of cultures and historical periods dealt with. The nineteenth-century focus also arose from a need to deal with a period in which diary writing was fairly common. Diary keeping was so well institutionalized in that century that many diaries from that period were written in blank books prepared for diarists, with the year stamped on the cover and pages or parts of pages dated.

Diaries from the nineteenth century are preferable to those of the twentieth for ethical reasons. It seems inappropriate to report material from diaries never intended for publication, especially while the diarist's contemporaries are alive. These ethical considerations are explored more fully in Appendix A. A practical reason for working with nineteenth-century diaries is that diaries rich in self-disclosure have not yet surfaced in great numbers in archives, and, among available twentieth-century diaries, a substantial proportion have restrictions on their use and on publication of their contents.

A crucial issue in using nineteenth-century diaries to revise twentieth-century grief theories is that the cultural world of the nineteenth century was different in many ways from our contemporary world. It was certainly a culturally diverse and changing world. For example, some people felt compelled to wear black when mourning, and others felt compelled not to (Farrell, 1980, p. 81). Nonetheless, it was a world that differed from the world of modern North Americans in mourning customs, religious beliefs, understandings of death, medical practices, life expectancy, infant mortality, funeral practices, life insurance, the use of hospitals, how death was discussed and how much, residential patterns, geographic mobility, and many other ways. But a case can be made that in crucial ways the diarists were like twentieth-century North Americans. People of the nineteenth century had the same basic needs (to eat, to be healthy, etc.) as people in the twentieth century, the same kinds of cultural institutions (marriage, parenthood, funerals, religion, a central government, etc.), and seemed generally to aspire to the same personal goals (happiness, a good life, self-respect and the respect of people around them, security for the future). Although there were some customs, for example, courtship customs, that were somewhat different from current practices, the great landmarks of the life cycle seem to have had the same impact on people then as now. And the things that upset people the most now seem to be the same things that upset them the most then. If my emotional reactions can be trusted, I can submit as evidence that the diaries I have read, including many that are not included in the sample, have often gripped me intensely; it has been easy to identify with the writers. The nineteenth-century diarists whose diaries I have used also seem to deal with grief in much the same way as the writers of published twentieth-century diaries I have read. I will not deny the possibility that in some crucial way the experiences of personal losses by people in the nineteenth century are different from those of people in the twentieth century, but I am unable to detect at present any difference that would invalidate the use of nineteenth-century diaries to understand grief in the twentieth century.

A case can be made that the basic character of close relationships does not vary among humans. The people one would be closest to and how that closeness would be expressed may vary, but that one must be close to some people appears to be a species characteristic. Thus, grief over relationship ending seems to be a species characteristic (Rosenblatt, Walsh, & Jackson, 1976). This is not to say that there are not differences between cultures and consequent great differences in products of the mind. But in the existence of close relationships, cultures must be similar. An earlier study of grief (Rosenblatt, Walsh, & Jackson, 1976) found a great deal of homogeneity in cultures in the area of expression of emotions of grief. It seemed clear, in that work, that useful cross-cultural comparisons of grief and mourning could be made.

There are some differences in the loss experiences of people in the United States and Canada in the nineteenth and twentieth centuries, for example, in the relative frequency of deaths of infants and children or in the relative frequency of home care for the terminally ill. There are certainly differences in customary mourning practices. Nonetheless, the basic experience of bereavement seems likely to have been very similar for people in both centuries. Ultimately, the question of whether nineteenth-century diaries can lead to new insight into twentieth-century grieving must be answered by readers who recognize the emotions expressed in this book, by researchers who find the implications of the diaries borne out in their studies, and by therapists who find that the therapeutic implications of the diary analyses lead to great gains in grief therapy.

The universe of diaries that was sampled has vague boundaries. Diaries used were written predominantly in Canada or in what is currently recognized as the United States (although many of the diarists who traveled in the western part of the United States before those areas became states or official territories considered themselves outside the United States and in a foreign land). Diary entries written in the nineteenth century (1801 through 1900) were used; entries written earlier or later were ignored. The temporal boundaries helped to keep the study manageable and focused, although they no doubt eliminated useful material from the study.

The universe of diaries is partly defined by published bibliographies, most notably the *Library of Congress National Union Catalog of Manuscript Collections*; by the lists compiled by William Matthews (1950, 1959, 1974); and by the published card catalogs of some of the great libraries. But these listings are often incomplete, as anyone can find when visiting manuscript repositories and wandering in library stacks; and these listings invariably include many works one would not call diaries, even when loosely defining the term. At a rough guess, there are between 25,000 and 100,000 published and unpublished U.S. and Canadian diaries available to scholars. I have looked at several thousands of these, and students working with me have surveyed hundreds for me.

Diaries written by famous people were avoided. Fame is, of course, a subjective matter. Anyone may be self-defined as famous. A person may have been famous locally in the nineteenth century but be obscure now, and a person who is now defined as famous may have had no prominence at all while alive. Nonetheless, it seemed reasonable to expect unpublished diaries of people who were apparently considered famous by themselves, their contemporaries, or their surviving descendants to have been censored (with pages torn out, volumes discarded). Published diaries of the famous might reasonably be expected to have sensitive material edited out. In such diaries, the absence of sentiments that could be embarrassing if made public (anger at God, relief that a loved one long ill had died) might be due to the diarist's reticence, or to editing by a descendant. Any diary may, of course, have passages altered or deleted because of embarrassing statements; but it seemed more likely that the problem would exist in the diary of a well-known person.

In addition, work with unpublished diaries of the famous is generally complicated by the large bulk of the papers in archival collections and controls put on publication of any part of those papers. Consequently, almost all of the diaries used in this study are diaries of the relatively obscure—people who did not, as far as can be determined, achieve great prominence among their contemporaries.

Only Lester Ward and Sanford Fleming, among all the diarists, seem to have achieved substantial fame. Ward's fame came long after the period covered by his diary, and there is no evidence that sensitive material was edited out of his published diary. Fleming was knighted after the period covered by the diary entries used in this study.

A diary was generally included in the sample as long as a loss was mentioned within three years of its occurrence, a date was given for the loss, and the relationship of the lost person to the diarist was indicated. For a diary to be included in the sample, a single loss (either death or separation) had to be mentioned only once if it was of a parent, spouse, child, sibling, grandchild more than one week old, stepchild, stepparent, or stepsibling. But, to protect against including diaries of compulsive obituary-recorders, for any other loss there had to be at least three mentions (and at least one of these mentions had to be for some reason other than that the diarist was a funeral officiant) before a diary would be included in the sample. Thus, a diary mentioning once the loss of a close relative or mentioning any other loss in three separate entries was included in the sample. These liberal criteria did not load the sample with the losses of people obsessed by news events (a violent local death, the death of someone famous); in fact, no death reported in the news was counted in this study as a personal loss. Although many diarists, for example, mentioned the assassination of President Lincoln, none mentioned Lincoln's death in three separate entries. From the evidence in the diaries, deaths of famous people and violent local deaths rarely affected people for more than a very brief time. Liberal criteria were used for counting a loss as a personal one because limiting the study to diaries that dealt in many entries with a loss might make the study one of very unusual people or very unusual losses. Some of the diaries in the sample have very few words devoted to loss.

Most (46 of 56) of the diaries in the sample were unpublished. Many published diaries lack loss material, though such material might have been in the original, unedited version. In fact, many published diaries with loss material are either so heavily edited or edited with so little information given on what was deleted that the passages cannot be trusted to reflect the diarist's grief in a valid way. For a scholar who wants quantitative data on "frequency of mentions of the person lost through death or separation," edited diaries are of little value. Consequently, most of the diaries in the sample were obtained from manuscript repositories. For two of the ten published diaries in the sample, those of Elkanah Walker and Mary Walker, the original manuscript or a copy of the original manuscript was checked, and the analyses involving those diaries include some fragments of loss-related material that were edited out of the published versions.

Among diaries that might have been used but were not were diaries with handwriting that defied reading, diaries with restrictions on their use, diaries that gave only retrospective accounts of losses experienced years before, and diaries that never gave sufficient information about the persons lost (most commonly omitting information on the relationship to the diarist of the person lost). It is possible that some of the dairies looked at had relevant material that was missed in skimming, particularly diaries covering long time spans in difficult handwriting. Thus, the sample includes 100 percent of the legible, loss-reporting diaries looked at, roughly 2.5 percent of all the diaries looked at.

The rarity of useful diaries raises serious questions about the oddity of the sample of diarists studied. Loss was common in the lives of people in the nineteenth century, and untimely losses were more common than in twentieth-century lives, what with frequent migration, high infant and child death rates, dreadful medical care, unsafe water, epidemics of cholera, typhoid, smallpox, and other diseases now controlled, and a very high accident rate (particularly involving horses and trains). It seems safe to assume that most nineteenth-century diarists who failed to mention losses experienced them. Perhaps, then, the diary was not, for many diarists, a place to record loss or feelings about loss; for them the diary had other functions. That seems true of the writers of many of the travel, immigration, or Gold Rush diaries; their diaries were most often logs of miles traveled and of campsites, or extended letters to send back home (in which case the bond of relationship may be seen by a scholar of grief, but feelings about the loss and, usually, the identity of the people left behind were not disclosed). Many Civil War diaries seem to have been written with journalistic objectivity or with the terseness of a log of orders and troop movements, so even in a situation where the diarist may have lost many close colleagues, one finds little if any mention of loss in the diary.

Perhaps the diarists who told little of losses controlled their grief by distancing it (not writing about it, not speaking of it). An effort was made to avoid bias against controlled diarists through use of any diary that mentioned loss of a close relative once or some other kind of loss at least three times. But it seems clear (especially where auxiliary documents such as letters or family genealogies could be checked) that some diarists simply avoided dealing with losses. It is also possible that much diary keeping is done by people who have no close relationships or who are young and have experienced few losses.

In the sample of 56 diarists, 26 were female and 30 were male. The median diarist age at first entry on which notes were made (not necessarily the first entry the diarist made) is 28.5 years of age. At least 11 of the diaries were kept 25 or more years, with the longest duration being 42 years. Occupationally, the diarists were quite diverse, and many held a number of different occupations over the span of the diary. A tabulation of principal occupations during the span of the diary indicates that 12 of the diarists were primarily farmers or, in a few cases, plantation operators, although many other diarists were living in households that raised some crops and kept domesticated animals. Five diarists were clergymen, and 15 were housewives (four as farm or plantation wives and four as wives of clergymen). Three diarists were retired, and for seven no occupation could be identified. Among the 14 other diarists no other occupation was represented by more than two cases.

The losses tabulated from the 56 diarists consisted of 140 deaths, including the death of a pet dog, and 178 separations. In some analyses of grief reported in this volume, the death of the dog is included. The number of deaths and separations tabulated from each dairy can be found in Appendix B: The Diarists.

The accompanying tabulation indicates the decade of first entry for the materials used. Concentration of the material in the middle of

Decade of First Entry for Parts of Diaries Used in the Sample

1801-1810	2
1811-1820	4
1821-1830	1
1831-1840	8
1841-1850	11
1851-1860	14
1861-1870	9
1871-1880	2
1881-1890	3
1891-1900	2
Total	56

the century is accounted for by a number of factors. There were fewer people to do writing at the beginning of the century, and it is more likely that older material may have been lost or may have deteriorated beyond rescue. Material from the last few decades of the century may still not have surfaced, and it may be less likely to surface because it is less interesting to archivists, historians, and publishers. Although the oldest material was more fragile (and hence more tempting to reject with a fast skimming), handwriting, vocabulary, and syntax were no more demanding for the early material than for the more recent. The archives used may have been relatively strong in Civil War diaries and in diaries dealing with the overland rush to the west that began in the 1840s. At any rate, the concentration of material in the middle of the century makes the sample unambiguously of that century.

Are Diarists Odd People?

Obviously a diarist has to be able to write, and so the sample being studied is biased in the direction of educated people (cf. Vinovskis, 1976, p. 290). But some people in the sample were just barely literate. The diarist also needs economic resources sufficient to provide a writing implement and material on which to write, though some diarists in the sample reported the purchase of a new pencil as though it was a major economic transaction (which it may have been), and some diaries were written on paper scraps or in the margins of salvaged books (including the margins of diaries kept years previously by the diarist or by a relative). The diarist needs some spare time and energy, which means, perhaps, that people with seasonal occupations (such as members of farming families), people who were relatively well-to-do, or people who could organize their time well are overrepresented among diarists. Diarists need a certain amount of egocentrism, enough to be interested in recording some aspects of the world they experience, though some diarists rarely mentioned themselves. Perhaps some diarists lacked a confidant or used diary keeping to get some emotional distance from the people with whom they lived. The list of possible differences between diarists and other people could be quite long, but it remains speculative. Research is needed that compares diarists and nondiarists.

The research would be particularly difficult to do on people of the nineteenth century.

Diarists may differ in their grief reactions from other people in two prominent ways. Diarists may be more prone than the rest of humanity to experience anniversary reactions. That is, they may be more conscious of the dates when things occurred, and this consciousness may mean that the anniversaries of separations and deaths have a bigger impact in the lives of diarists. Also, diarists may be more familiar with literary material dealing with losses, including poetry, sermons, and "consolation" literature (Douglas, 1974). See, for example, Mary Richardson Walker's reference to Cowper in a quote near the end of chapter 5. Familiarity with literary sources may influence written reactions to losses in a way that suppresses culturally unusual reports, producing reactions that fit cultural expectations.

2

Do Diaries Seem to Tell the Truth about Diarist Grief?

Can one assume that the diaries in the sample studied accurately report the events of the diarists' lives and their inner experiences? In exploring the value of the diary data, perhaps the best place to begin is with the first entries reporting loss. Do these entries seem to tell the truth?

The First Entry of Loss

The word "loss" is used to cover both deaths and separations. All the separations were due to one person moving away temporarily or permanently from another. The most common separations arose from migration from one part of the United States to another, from one part of Canada to another, and from Europe to North America. There were no divorces among the 56 diarists in the sample. The use of the term "loss" does not imply that diarists necessarily experienced a death or a separation as a source of deprivation, grief, or reduction in satisfaction of wants. The term "loss" is used only to describe a permanent or temporary ending to a relationship. People studying grief, particularly since theoretical work by Bowlby (1961), have considered all losses to have elements in common, so in the perspective of recent work on grief there is nothing unusual about studying grief for separations at the same time as grief for deaths. It seems easier, moreover, to understand one kind of loss in the perspective of the other. Understanding what it means to work through an irreversible loss due to death is easier, for example, if one knows something about responses to potentially reversible losses due to separation.

The first account of a loss often overshadows most other entries in a diary—in terms of length, descriptive detail, emotional intensity, self-disclosure, and questioning about the meaning of life and the diarist's future. This is true even for the diary of Edward Bolivar Drew. His entries were typically more laconic than the following passages.

* * * * * * *

"Milton & Sarah [diarjst's wife] leave for the east—Take them to Winona with the colts and Lord's light wagon. Staid in town till sometime after dark to see them off. Awful lonesome ride home & home a lonesome place."

Diary of Edward Bolivar Drew. Unpublished manuscript, Minnesota Historical Society, entry of October 18, 1859.

* * *

"I am compelled to chronicle here the sadest [sic] event of my life. Nothing could have happened to me that would have been more so. My wife was taken sick about mid night. About 6 o clk her child was born. About 9 she died. The poor child is alive & well. O what a day. . . . what is this world to me now? Were it not for my four poor helpless motherless children. They must be taken care of."

Diary of Edward Bolivar Drew, entry of March 7, 1868.

* * *

"My poor baby is dead. Died about 4 o'clk P.M. Ages 6 mos. & 9 days. First frost this morning. John G. Laird pays me $50.00 & takes his note. Let Bosink have $50.00 agreeable to promise. Get Bundy to dig the grave."

Diary of Edward Bolivar Drew, entry of September 16, 1868.

* * * * * * *

It is not always obvious what the first entry containing an account of a loss is or what it represents. There is the problem of entries made at some time after an event. Some first entries of loss seem to have been made days, weeks, or even months after the loss. It is plausible that for some people the shock of a loss or the preoccupation with dealing with the tasks required by the death or separation would delay the writing of the account of the loss. But if a loss is described some time after it has occurred, the delay may mean that the feelings reported in the entry are not those of a new grief but of a grief that has been changed by grief work, or perhaps of a grief more distinct or more strong than that accompanying an initial shock reaction. In delaying the writing of a first entry of loss, one's grief may be magnified through repeated review of events before the writing, and a delayed account is more likely to contain ideas and descriptions acquired from other people.

Delayed Realization

In theory, another problem in identifying the first entry of loss is the problem of delayed realization of loss. (See discussion in the next chapter of Lindemann's development of the theory of grief work.) The delay in realization may arise from feelings of shock, from ego defenses that protect one against the full realization of what one has lost, or simply from insufficient imagination. If there is such a delay in realization, the first entry reporting the loss may not be, in terms of emotion, the first entry of loss. Some subsequent entry that reflects a full realization of the loss may be the first entry. There seem to be, however, only three or possibly four instances among the 318 deaths and separations reported by diarists in the sample in which a delay in realization may have occurred.

In one instance of delayed realization, Alfred F. Armstrong, a Union soldier in the Civil War, reported his mother's death in an entry dated September 25, 1863. The next day he wrote: "Bright & pleasant—feeling sad and lonely. My heart is full. I have begun to realize *'I am Motherless'*. Oh! What an affliction. I can hardly sit still thinking of her all day. . . ." (Unpublished manuscript, Archives of Ontario, Toronto).

After Mary White's daughter Fannie died February 29, 1844, White wrote in the first entry following the death, the entry of March 10: ". . . I am just beginning to feel her loss & each day as I see the group of little ones around me & hear their cries raised in tuneful praise I feel that one is absent, that our sweetest singer is gone & can scarcely realize that it is forever but seem to feel that she will soon again be here & mingle her voice with those who are sad without her. But I know that these are vain thoughts. She will no longer return to us, but we shall go to her. . . ." (Diary of Mary White, unpublished manuscript, Huntington Library).

Mrs. Charles C. Carpenter was in Labrador when she learned from a letter received June 12, 1863, of the death of her brother. Seventeen entries after the initial entry of June 12, she wrote about her brother George that "I realize more & more each day what is gone. . . ." (Unpublished filmed manuscript, entry of June 28, 1863, Public Archives of Canada, Ottawa).

Diarist Understanding of When the Loss Occurred

A key problem in deciding what is the first entry of a loss is to determine when the diarist considered the loss to have occurred. It is possible to feel all the pain and horror of a loss at a time before or after what a neutral observer would count as the time of loss. If the diarist knew days or weeks in advance that a separation would occur or that someone had a fatal illness, what is the first entry of loss? Is it the first entry reporting the separation or death, or is it the first entry that indicates a separation or a death is to occur? Is it even a matter of one point in time versus another? It may be a peculiarity of Western civilization, with its calendars and clocks, in which births, deaths, and separations are recorded to the minute, to consider a loss to have begun at a specific point in time. Most people in history might have experienced the beginnings of losses over substantial time periods. Or perhaps various aspects of a loss have been felt, by many people, to have begun at different times. Thus, the first realizations of loss might have occurred over a substantial period of time, perhaps extending well into the period after a separation or death had occurred (see the discussion below of first returnings to places that were important in a relationship ended by separation or death).

It seems to be an open question what the first entry of loss actually is. However, all diarists seem to have written with a specific point of loss in mind. It is conceivable that some experienced the loss differently, but none wrote of such a difference. Perhaps nineteenth-century North American diarists, like twentieth-century North Americans, thought in terms of specific times for events and experiences. It would be helpful to have a more probing examination of the matter—for example, answers to careful questions put at many points in time. In the absence of such data it seems reasonable to call the first entry that reports the actual occurrence of a death or separation the "first entry of loss."

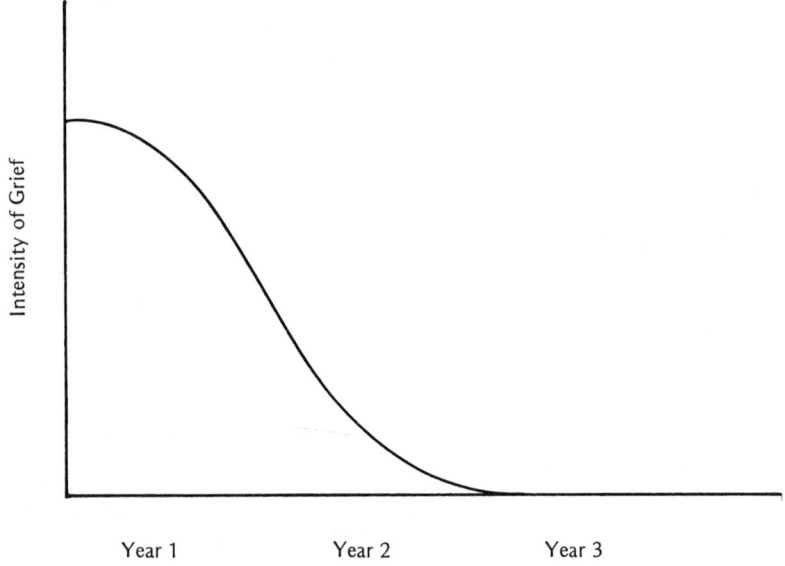

Figure 2.1

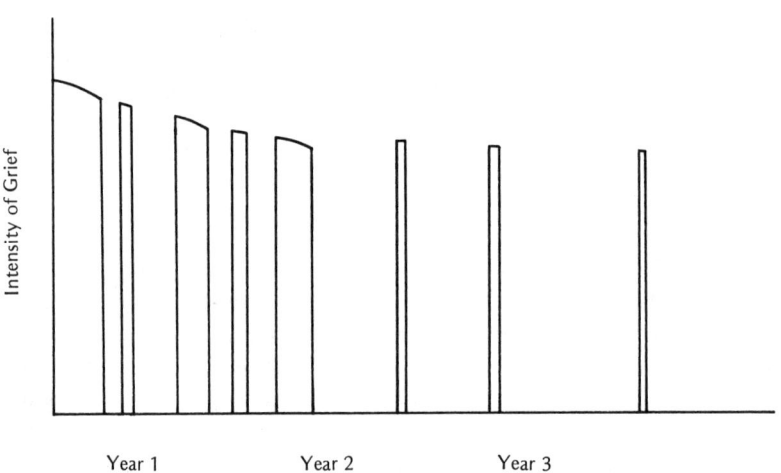

Figure 2.2

Patterning of Grief

Although grief is often talked of as something that gradually changes (and tables such as 6.1 and 6.2 may encourage such viewpoints), the detailed data from the diaries seem to indicate that grief comes and goes recurrently. It does not seem, in the thoughts and feelings of the typical diarist, to wane gradually but to be absent some of the time and present some of the time. The diary data show that, rather than grief or thoughts of the lost person becoming steadily weakened, times of remembering alternate with times of no mention of the lost. A graphic representation of the time course of grief or remembering a lost person would look not like Figure 2.1 but like Figure 2.2. The intensity, duration, and some qualitative aspects of a grief probably change over time, but the peaks of emotional intensity, even after several years have passed, may still be quite elevated (cf. Glick, Weiss, & Parkes, 1974; Goin, Burgoyne, & Goin, 1979; Parkes, 1972, p. 57, 1975c; Pollock, 1961). In fact, for some losses normal grief work may leave one operating in the shadow of grief permanently (Goin, Burgoyne, & Goin, 1979; Peppers & Knapp, 1980, chap. 5; Silver & Wortman, 1980), with a sense of one's loss present often and with occasional bouts of relatively intense feelings of grief.

The following diary excerpts, all drawn from the second and third year of bereavement for a spouse who had died, express an intensity of feeling which seems to refute the notion that grief feelings simply wane over a year or at most two years. Each entry quoted, except the second one by Burge, was preceded by entries containing no grief for the spouse who had died. These entries provide anecdotal support for the notion that grief comes and goes recurrently.

* * * * * * *

"Have been reading over some of my old letters to my beloved husband, & been ready to long that the bond may be sundered wh. holds me to earth, & detains me from *him*. . . . Reading these letters (a thing wh. I have never trusted myself to do before) seems to have revived all the exclusiveness & intenseness of my love for him I once called *husband*. I am so filled with a sense of the fearfulness of my loss & the awful chasm made in my heart & affections that all on earth seems a void without him. 'I sit alone as a swallow upon the house top.' My heart turns away from all human helpers. Oh how bitter was that cup of trembling wh. God put into my hands! . . ."

Diary of Susan Mansfield Huntington, unpublished manuscript, Sterling Memorial Library, Yale University, entry of June 26, 1822, thirty-four months after her husband had died. Her diary had contained no expression of grief for her husband in the ten months preceding this entry.

* * *

". . . How many things occur day by day to remind me of the irreparable loss of her that was dearer to me than all the world beside. Twenty-one years ago this evening we were united in the Holy Bonds of Matrimony & for twenty long years enjoyed each others society, as happy a married couple as ever lived on this wicked earth, but alas how changed is all now, she gone home to rest while I lonely & sad plod along the journey of life."

Diary of Dustin G. Cheever, unpublished manuscript, Whitewater Regional Historical Center, Wisconsin State Historical Society, entry of January 4, 1874, one year and three days after the death of his wife. There had been three diary entries without grief for his spouse since the last entry with grief, which was written on December 31, 1873.

* * *

". . . To-day has been very warm & as I sat in my lonely porch tonight, how vividly was brought to mind the night of two years since when I had every thing packed & ready to start home to Maine with my poor dear sick husband. How I dreaded the journey, how I feared the consequences that might be & how calmly & cheerfully he said 'I want to go & you must go with me.' And when I told him my fears he said, 'Well, suppose I should die, will I not be as near Heaven there as here? And you can have my poor dust brought back.' And . . . the same moon that now shines so calmly upon his grave & me in my loneliness shone upon us together in the porch talking it all over. . . ." Entry of May 24, 1860.

"This night finds me solitary & alone in my room, a boarder in my own house. How strange & lonely everything is! Sadai is in Atlanta visiting at Dr. Crichton's. Oh, how I miss her & how I miss the dear, good husband that left me over a year ago for his home with Jesus, but the days are passing swiftly on when I shall meet him there. Happy meeting, blessed day. I have been very busy these holidays arranging my house for Dr. Haygood, putting away & fixing up my things so I have not lived over & dwelled upon the past so much as usual. . . ." Entry of December 31, 1874.

Diary of Dolly Lunt Burge (1962, pp. 66, 133). Burge was widowed three times. In the first diary excerpt quoted here, she expressed grief for her second husband, who had been dead for 18 months. Her most recent previous expression of grief for him appeared approximately a year earlier in her diary. In the second diary excerpt quoted here, she expressed grief for her third husband, who had been dead for 15 months.

* * *

"I was home alone at Eve, fearfully alone Ma and you cannot come back. It was cruel to take you so, so soon. . . ." Entry of July 4, 1896, in the 29th month since the death of his wife ("Ma"). The last previous entry with grief for "Ma" was written 90 entries before this one.

". . . I think of Ma so much, & the horror of her taking never leaves me. Why should that condition come to her. Why should she keep it secret so long. What would have prevented it." Entry of July 24, 1896, in the 30th month since the death of his wife. No grief was expressed for her in the nineteen entries between July 4 and July 24. When Snow said that the horror of his wife's death never left him, he may have meant either that he thought of her continually or that, although he did not think of her continually, when he did think of her he felt the horror of her death.

Diary of Corwin R. Snow, unpublished manuscript, State University of Iowa Libraries, Iowa City.

* * * * * * *

When Do Diarists Think about Their Losses?

One could argue that the apparent fact of discontinuous grieving is an artifact of the process of diary keeping. Perhaps the diarists always thought of people they had lost but only budgeted a fraction of their entries to mentioning the lost.

It may be that grief did not change over time, only that diary writing changed. A diarist's sentiments might have remained constant, although he or she resisted writing the same sentiment in entry after entry. But no diarist wrote that redundant information would be omitted from his or her diary. In fact, many diarists seem to have had no fear of redundancy; one of the trials of studying diaries is that they are typically repetitive.

Despite the apparent redundancy, diarists may have withheld clues to their grief. A diarist may be willing to be redundant about weather but not about feelings. Did any diarist ever say something like "I never stop thinking of the lost person?" Three diarists did at some point after the first month of grieving: Corwin Snow and I. O. Krohnke, each of whom was grieving for his wife, and George Wright, who was grieving for a daughter. Snow, for example, wrote on September 13, 1895, 17 months after the death of his wife, "Ma," that "I think of Ma all the time" (quoted from unpublished manuscript, State University of Iowa Libraries, Iowa City). On the anniversary of his wife's death Krohnke wrote: ". . . it does not go a day when I do not remember her, and I feel as if her memory will be holy for me all my life. . . ." (Diary of I. O. Krohnke, unpublished typescript translation, Wisconsin State Historical Society, entry of November 11, 1850). Wright wrote on April 16, 1879, four months after his 11-year-old daughter died, "Ah Nelly, Nelly. You have left a blank that nothing hereafter can fill up, and you do not even visit me in dreams of the night. It seems strange. Perhaps you will come when I cease to think of you all the day long!" (quoted from unpublished manuscript, Public Archives of Canada, Ottawa).

In the case of Wright, who died in November 1879, there was no mention of always thinking of the lost beyond that April entry. For Krohnke, too, there was no evidence that remembering was constant; perhaps what he meant was that on a typical day he had a fleeting memory of his wife. That might not be at all unusual for people who have lost a spouse, but it is not the same as daily grieving. For Snow, however, whose diary seems the most obsessively focused on a specific lost person of any diary in the sample, the entries provide a sense of always thinking of the lost and of persistent grief. Snow's entries show a higher proportion of mentions of the deceased and of grief for the deceased running through the third year of loss than does the average diary. His diary thus reflects the obsessive concern which he confessed to but which he said he did not always write about.

It may well be that the typical diarist thought often of a lost person who was nonetheless mentioned only occasionally in the diary, but there is no evidence in the diaries that the typical diarist was not disclosing much private grieving. The relationship between thought and written diary entries is a crucial issue and one that would be interesting to address with other data—letters, for example. But other data were lacking for most of the diaries, and it must be assumed, without external data, that the diary record parallels the mental and emotional state of the diarist.

Occasions for Grief

Another way of determining whether the data are accurate records of the diarists' internal states is to ask whether the entries with grief for the lost seem random or patterned. Patterning would suggest meaning. In fact, the diarists' thoughts of lost persons do not seem to have arisen spontaneously; they seem typically to have been caused.

To expand on the definition provided at the beginning of chapter 1, the following definition was used in assessing whether grief was present in a diary entry: Grief is defined as expressed feelings of sorrow, loss of interest in work, depression, being unable to eat or sleep, or other signs of distress about the specific person or persons lost, or expressing either a desire to reunite on earth with the lost or joy at hearing from the lost. The last two elements in the definition mean that, except in the case of spiritists (people who believed they could and did communicate with the spirit of the deceased), somewhat different things were being counted for grief over death versus grief over separation. The assumption is that it is a mistake to look for the same things in comparing death grief and separation grief. The words used in the two kinds of grief must inevitably be different some of the time.

When diary entries with grief for a lost person are examined, grief seems far more often than not to have arisen from a particular stimulus. Some stimuli occurred for grief over both deaths and separations. Other stimuli were unique to deaths or to separations. For most statements of grief over a loss (89%) there seems a cause or occasion. That is, there is some information in the entry containing the grief that provides a plausible reason for the grief to be occurring. Reasons common to both deaths and separations are:

1. Reports of the loss — 13% of all entries with grief. The first entry in which a diarist reported a loss seems often to be a sort of announcement to herself or himself or a statement of detailed information intended to be kept permanently. Although grief in these entries seems authentic, in some cases the grief statement may also reflect the etiquette of making an announcement or a record of loss. It might seem disrespectful not to express grief.

2. Special dates, such as birthdays; days exactly one or more weeks, months, or years after the wedding of the lost; holidays of special importance (December 31 and January 1, because they seem to be, for many diarists, times for taking stock of life; Christmas; July 4) — 5% of all grief entries.

3. Days exactly one or more weeks, months, or years after death, parting, or terminal illness crisis — 3% of all grief entries.

4. A death or parting involving someone other than the lost person — 3% of all grief entries.

5. The diarist's being alone — 2% of all grief entries.

6. Occurrence of a significant family event—e.g., a birth, wedding, property loss, an achievement, reunion with a family member other than the lost—1% of all grief entries.
7. Someone's mention of the lost; news of the lost person received or not received when it was reasonable to expect it—1% of all grief entries.
8. Sunday or Sabbath (a time for stock-taking, for family togetherness, and for religious reflection)—4% of all grief entries.
9. Someone seen who looked like the lost or reminded the diarist of the lost—1% of all grief entries.
10. Dreams of the lost person—1% of all grief entries.

Reasons commonly associated with grief over a death but not over a separation:

11. Burial, probate, stone dedication, legal work due to the death, autopsy, death watch, expecting remains to arrive, body preparation for funeral or burial, funeral, funeral visitation, telling others of just-occurred death—5% of all grief entries.
12. Seance, seance sought, decision not to hold seance, seance not possible—6% of all grief entries.

Reasons commonly associated with grief over a separation but not over a death:

13. Mail received from lost or concerning lost—23% of all grief entries.
14. Mail not received when it could reasonably be expected—8% of all grief entries.
15. Diarist wrote to lost—3% of all grief entries.
16. Reunion with lost expected—1% of all grief entries.

The tabulations are a bit rough because a few entries were counted in more than one category. The 16 occasions for grief over the lost encompass roughly 80% of entries with grief over lost people. The occasions are distributed differently for different diarists, depending in part on whether the major losses in the diarist's life were deaths or separations, but also on other factors. Some diarists, for example, dwelt on birthdays, one on seances, and several on mail sent, received, or expected but not received.

There may be other ways of seeing any given entry than the way it was categorized here, although the possibility of tabulating an entry in more than one category may make these categories less arbitrary.

Perhaps one would have needed an interview with each diarist on each occasion of apparent grief to understand fully what was going on. A diarist might have been alone on a Sunday and expressed grief for a lost relative, but the actual stimulus might have been something read that day, something never mentioned in the diary entry. To complicate matters, not every occasion of a type that sometimes led to a report of grief over a lost person led to a grief report. Nonetheless, causes seem often to have been clear, and judging by what they said, the diarists often thought that they knew the causes of grief experiences. Consider the following examples.

* * * * * * *

". . . were able to sit in our old pew. I could not help thinking of my dear parents and before I could stop myself was crying bitterly. . . ." Diary of Eleanora Hallen, unpublished typed extracts, Archives of Ontario, Toronto, entry of January 18, 1846.

* * *

"I think of Henry every time I sit at table and see his place is vacant. It is lonely but I am glad he is doing well, and will try to be brave. . . ."

Diary of Emily Hawley Gillespie, October 2, 1883. Unpublished manuscript, Iowa State Historical Society, Iowa City.

* * *

"Thanksgiving Day, and a lonely one for us. This is the sixth Thanksgiving that has passed since our family were all together. Three of the number are gone forever, John, Gramp [diarist's father], and Anna." Diary of Mary Dodge Woodward, entry of November 27, 1884 (Woodward, 1937, p. 56). There are similar entries for Thanksgiving Day 1885 and 1886.

* * * * * * *

One of the types of stimuli that set off memories of the lost is sometimes of special significance in clinical evaluation of grief—dates that are loss anniversaries (type 3 in the list above). Anniversary reactions are sometimes taken as a sign of pathology by clinicians who work with the bereaved, yet anniversary reactions are not uncommon among the diarists. Thirteen of the 44 diarists who kept a diary around the anniversary of at least one loss noted, with grief, dates that occurred roughly one, two, or three years after a terminal illness, loss, or burial. Perhaps anniversary reactions are more common for diarists; their keeping of dated records and their ability to check back to see what happened on a given date may make anniversaries more salient for them. But the noting of a significant date may also be a product of Western culture, a culture with calendars and sanctioned observation of specific dates such as holidays and birthdays. From such a cultural viewpoint, it seems at least as strange that one would not note the anniversary of a significant loss in one's life as that one would.

Seemingly Uncaused Mentions of Loss

A critic might argue that the apparent stimuli to grief over the lost are an investigator's speculations, not constructions of the diarists. I have found, however, that diary entries with grief over lost persons for which no cause is indicated occur in a pattern that supports the validity of the analysis of grief stimuli. These seemingly uncaused recurrences of grief for a lost person should be expected to occur soon after the date of the loss. The diarist would still be struggling with a myriad of adjustments to the loss, and if the loss was of someone who lived with the diarist, there would be reminders of the lost person wherever the diarist turned. It seems reasonable to expect that, as adjustments were made and as many unremarkable stimuli in the immediate environment became less associated with the lost person, diary entries containing seemingly uncaused grief for the lost would become less frequent. There would be periods in which the diarist did not think of the lost person. Then, when the diarist did think of him or her, the thought would typically be set off by specific, identifiable stimuli. That is what the data seem to show for grief over the first three years of loss, but the pattern is less clear for the first three months of loss.

Tabulations were made for the first three months and for the first three years following a loss as to whether there was an increase, a decrease, or no change in the proportion of entries with seemingly uncaused grief over the lost. The analysis sums over all losses for a given diarist, so each diarist could contribute up to three comparisons for the first three months (first with second and third months, second with third) and for the first three years (first with second and third years, second with third). The analysis is summarized in Table 2.1. Not all diarists are represented in the table because some had entries in none or only one of the first three months of loss and some had entries during only one of the years following the loss.

In the analysis in Table 2.1, almost all the instances of no difference in the two rows of numbers (38 of 39) occur where the two months or two years being compared lack any seemingly uncaused mention of the lost person. Examination of Table 2.1 indicates that the proportion of seemingly uncaused mentions is greater in the

Table 2.1. Relative Proportion of Seemingly Uncaused Mentions of Lost Persons

	Greater Proportion in Earlier than in Later Period	Same Proportion in Earlier and in Later Period	Smaller Proportion in Earlier than in Later Period
First Three Months	13	24	9
First Three Years	22	15	2

Note: Each tally in this table represents a comparison for a specific diarist between one month and another or between one year and another.

earlier months of the first three and in the earlier years of the first three following the occurrence of loss. The effect is, however, much weaker in the first three months. It stands to reason that in the second and third month following a loss seemingly uncaused grief for a lost person might occur in proportionately more entries than in a second or third year following a loss. In the initial period, apparently spontaneous recurrences of grief (or recurrences in response to almost any stimulus, however subtle) might be more common.

It may be too extreme to call all the occasions for grief over a lost person "causes." Does a seance cause one to grieve for the lost, or does the grief cause the seance? Does writing a letter to a separated person call forth grief for the person, or does the grief call forth the letter writing? Does what seems like the report of a cause represent the diarist's search for a personal explanation of the eruption of grief for a lost person? Occasionally a diarist makes clear that a memory has bubbled up without any obvious "cause." For example, Mary Dodge Woodward, in an entry for June 7, 1885, wrote: "I have been thinking of home and my absent loved ones today for some unknown reason. Perhaps it is because we did not get our mail on Saturday" (Woodward, 1937, p. 84). The dairy data do not always allow a confident use of a concept like "cause." Perhaps "occasion" might be a less pretentious term for the context in which a lost person is mentioned.

Conclusions: Data Validity

The analysis of first entries suggests that it is probably not a mistake to identify specific first entries of a loss. This is important both in terms of plotting grief over time (one can begin the plot at a specific point) and in analyzing the dynamics of grief (one need not worry about dynamics based on a conception of loss as spread out over time or of divisible loss, with each part perceived as beginning at a different point in time).

Although the absence of convergent data from other sources leaves one uncertain about the validity of the grief data over time, the patterning of those data suggests that they have some meaning. The diarists do not seem merely to have given a small random sample in their diaries of a much larger stock of private thoughts and feelings. That there seem to be "occasions" for most expressions of grief and that the grief entries without "occasions" seem to be early ones, particularly in the first year of loss, suggests that if there were much spontaneous grief for the lost it would appear in the diaries. Instead, it seems that after the initial period of loss most grief experiences are linked to specific, diary-identified events.

Conclusions: Dynamics of Grief

The probe of the validity of the data points to some conclusions that can be drawn about the dynamics of grief. The "occasions" data, with most diary entries containing grief (particularly after the initial period of loss) being linked to specific occasions, suggest that grief processes, like other thought processes, are linked to external events. Thus, grief is to some extent out of one's control; events and other people can stimulate it. It also suggests that one can control one's grief in part by avoiding certain places and people and preoccupying oneself at certain times. What the diarists say about self-control of grief is explored fully in Chapter 9. As the discussion in the next chapter points out, the central theory in contemporary writings about grief, the theory of grief work, has room for the notion of recurrent grieving set off by reminders. The theory, which speaks of detaching memories, ideas, and behavior patterns from someone lost through death, implies that the detaching occurs when memories, ideas, and behavior patterns arise that call for some sort of awareness of the deceased. Thus, any reminder that elicits memories, ideas, and behavior patterns not previously detached fully from the deceased would set off new or intensified grief. This analysis would refine the perspective developed in the present chapter by suggesting that it is primarily external events not faced before that would unexpectedly and at some time distant from the loss set off grief when one thought one had finished with it.

In addition, the "occasions" data suggest that even after one thinks one has finished with a loss, occasions arise (dates, mentions by other persons, and so on) that bring the lost person to mind again. If one can extrapolate from the data for the first three years of loss in the diaries, a bereaved person and people close to the bereaved can never be sure that the work of dealing with a loss has ended. Thoughts of the lost always have the potential of returning; novel reminders appear, and feelings of bereavement can never be counted as ended.

Rules of thumb for identifying people with pathological grief over a death often are based on the assumption that grief follows a smoothly declining path and that nonrecurrence is normal (see, for example, Burgess & Lazare, 1976, p. 100). Yet the diary data seem to indicate that people who are normal by commonly accepted standards—able to function at work and in relationships, not complaining of constant depression, etc.—may often grieve for the lost some years after a death, at holidays and anniversaries or when faced with some other reminder. After several years, these thoughts may be rare (see Table 6.1), but their presence seems understandable and not obviously pathological.

3

The Theory of Grief Work

Almost any theory that deals with human emotion, behavior, interaction, or cognitive process can be a theory of grief. Some theories used in this book are not specifically grief theories—for example, theories of memory, emotional control, and family systems. However, a substantial part of this book involves wrestling with and applying various versions of what seems to be the major theory of grief—the theory of grief work. This theory is typically recognized as having its origins in Freud's "Mourning and Melancholia" (1959, originally published in 1917), an essay written to illuminate pathological depression (melancholia), although the theory can be traced to earlier writings of Freud (Pollock, 1961).

This chapter offers a selective overview of the core ideas of the theory of grief work and its derivatives. It does not trace the origins of all the versions of this theory, nor does it catalog the many versions of the theory. The articles and books cited in the bibliography, however, provide a good sampling of the many versions of the theory of grief work.

Freud's "Mourning and Melancholia"

Freud's "Mourning and Melancholia" (1959) offers the following view of grief:

"The testing of reality, having shown that the loved object no longer exists, requires forthwith that all the libido shall be withdrawn from its attachments to the object. Against this demand a struggle of course arises—it may be universally observed that man never willingly abandons a libido-position, not even when a substitute is already beckoning to him. . . . The task is now carried through bit by bit, under great expense of time and cathectic energy, while all the time the existence of the lost object is continued in the mind. Each single one of the memories and hopes which bound the libido to the object is brought up and hyper-cathected, and the detachment of the libido from it is accomplished. Why this process of carrying out the behest of reality bit by bit, which is in the nature of a compromise, should be so extraordinarily painful is not at all easy to explain in terms of mental economics. . . . The fact is, however, that when the work of mourning is completed the ego becomes free and uninhibited again (1959, p. 154).

The grief process as Freud analyzed it is a slow, intensely demanding struggle. What Freud called "memories" and "hopes" might reasonably include behavior patterns and plans involving the lost, and one's view of reality as it involves the lost person. Thus, it seems consistent with the Freudian view that the more ways in which one is connected to someone who is lost—the more memories, hopes, interaction sequences, and so on—the more grief work there is to do. The implications of this aspect of the theory of grief work are developed most fully in Chapter 8. The "work" of the process is the struggle to detach oneself, one's memories, and one's hopes from the person who has been lost. It is "work" in the sense of demanding energy, effort, and a willingness to face up to pain. One must do the detaching to end one's grief; there is no alternate route to that ending.

What did Freud mean by the ego becoming "free and uninhibited again"? He probably did not mean that one forgets the person one has lost. Rather, he meant that one can think, remember, and behave in areas that once involved the person now dead without feeling strong grief and without any sense that one should act as though the lost person were still alive. That is, one is now free to act as though the dead person no longer exists as a living being. That freedom includes the freedom to think well of oneself and to engage in a minimum of self-reproach in response to one's loss (Ricouer, 1970, pp. 130-132).

The diary data provide many examples of memories not forgotten but altered in emotional significance so that the diarist could function without strong grief and without feeling compelled to think of a dead person as still alive. Here are two examples from the diary of Linka Keyser (1952, pp. 254-255). The two excerpts quoted each deal with the death of the diarist's sister Waleska (Hexa). First news of Hexa's death came around September 1, 1853.

* * * * * * *

". . . . For some time it was a sad experience indeed to omit the name of my Hexa whenever I wrote home to my sisters. Frequently I checked myself in my thoughts, and once or twice I almost wrote: 'Dear Sister Hexa,' at the head of the letter. . . ." Entry of March 4, 1854.

* * *

"It is exactly a year ago today since sister Waleska died—the beloved sister!— I think of thee very often, and frequently talk with thee. But that conversation is so strange, and I wonder why? No doubt I am too earthbound to commune with thee who already art with God in heaven. My thoughts seem always to revolve about things transitory. When the dear memories of the days we spent together rise up before me, I still remain earth-bound. . . ." Entry of June 30, 1854.

* * * * * * *

In these two passages, Keyser looked back on her earlier grief work ("Frequently I checked myself"). She had to break patterns of behavior (writing her sister's name in letters home) that were appropriate only as long as her sister was alive. Ten months after learning of her sister's death, she still thought often of her sister and had fantasy conversations with her, but with a sense that the relationship had been sundered.

Failure to Do Grief Work

A large proportion of the theorizing about grief that has followed "Mourning and Melancholia" has dealt with the pathologies that arise when grief work has not occurred or is incomplete or faulty. One can deduce from Freud's analysis that failure to do grief work may leave one too numb for the struggle the work requires, may leave one in the midst of the work, and, in either case, may leave one poorly organized to deal with a world without the lost person.

In the United States, perhaps the most influential theory about failures to carry out grief work was contained in Lindemann's (1944) description of symptom patterns and responses to treatment of victims and relatives of victims of the fire at the Cocoanut Grove night club. Following Freud, Lindemann wrote about grief work as the "emancipation from the bondage to the deceased, readjustment to the environment in which the deceased is missing, and the formation of new relationships." Lindemann's analysis provided a sense of "work" in the grief work process; he gave a sense of the energy absorbed by the loss as the bereaved person functioned with reduced zest and initiative.

In Lindemann's analysis, one pathology of grief was a holding back from entry into grief work. People he classified in this way seemed to hold back from expressing emotion, and that holding back was seen by Lindemann as a source of great tension and diversion of psychic energy. Once they became willing to "accept the grief process," Lindemann observed them to be much less tense and much more animated.

Another kind of grief work problem arose in people who were actually engaging in grief work but who found it so painful or so frightening that they feared loss of sanity, claimed to want to die, or considered terminating the work process by withdrawing from their familiar social and physical surroundings. In such cases, Lindemann reported that a psychiatric approach that supported and encouraged the work process was beneficial. Operating with the model of grief work in mind, Lindemann was able to push people to grieve and to work at detaching themselves from the deceased. In the diary material there are instances of all three "pathological" symptoms early in the grief process—fear of loss of sanity, wishing to die, and withdrawal from familiar social and physical surroundings. In every instance the bereaved diarist resumed grieving or continued grieving without psychiatric help. It may be that those alleged pathologies are relatively common early in bereavement and rarely are a permanent barrier to grief work.

Lindemann also wrote about so-called distorted reactions. The bereaved person might develop physical symptoms like those of the last illness of the deceased or of a recognized medical disease such as colitis or arthritis. Or the bereaved might develop psychological symptoms, such as progressive withdrawal from social contacts. The "distortion" is of the normal behavioral and emotional processes of grief work. However, it may be difficult to distinguish the so-called distorted reactions from normal reactions. Physical illness may be as much an expression of emotion as is depression or crying. And withdrawal from contacts seems consistent with the picture both Freud and Lindemann gave of the normal process of grief work, one in which energy and attention are absorbed by the work.

The most pathological reactions, according to Lindemann, were cases of extreme delay of onset of grief work and cases of extreme blocking of work on a particular loss (in some cases by grieving strongly for a prior loss). With diary material, it is always difficult to decide when blocking has occurred. Failure to mention grieving in the diary may not be indicative of failure to grieve. Discussion of losses in the distant past may indicate only that the diarist was thinking about mortality or putting the current grief in perspective, not that the most recent loss lacked primacy.

Finally, Lindemann extended the concept of grief work into the areas of anticipation of a loss and into other areas of loss than deaths (though that latter extension was foreshadowed in Freud's discussion of some cases of melancholia). Lindemann asserted that grief work can occur in anticipation of the actual fact of a loss, and also that grief work can occur with separation, even at the cost of having a hollow relationship when reunion occurs. Anticipatory grief is discussed in Chapter 4, and grief over death is compared with grief over separation in Chapter 6.

Another person who expanded the theory of grief work, with a focus on pathologies of the grief work process, was Geoffrey Gorer (1967). Gorer, working in Britain, carried out a large-scale survey and intensively interviewed 80 people in the survey sample. He extended the model of grief work by characterizing some states of arrested or incomplete work and by giving those states names. He wrote about two types of grieving which seemed more or less intense and permanent. One he called "mummification"; in it a person grieving for someone who is dead attempts to keep dwelling and life routine as they were before the death. Failure to change one's life routine would, of course, be a sign that grief work had not occurred or had not progressed very far.

The other type of permanent grief he labeled "despair." Characteristically, the people in despair seemed flat emotionally and were living in comparative isolation. The constellation of dulled emotion, social isolation, and strong feelings of grief could be characteristic of people in the midst of grief work and not necessarily in a state of permanent arrest of the process. Some of the so-called despair cases were people whose bereavement had begun as recently as 12 months before the interview (Jeffrey Lerner, personal communication). For them, few who write about grief would expect grief work not to be going on. To determine whether grieving is arrested or continuing may be impossible in a single interview, and whether 12 months, two years, or five years is sufficient time to allow normal grief work to be completed is not obvious.

The theory of grief work should be augmented by some theoretical notion about the rate of grief work, based on the time needed to disconnect hopes and memories in different situations of loss. It seems obvious that people who are unemployed and living alone would have less opportunity to do the grief work required by a loss. In general, the more isolated one is and the less pressure one is under to produce or to interact as though the loss had occurred, the slower the grief work process can be expected to be. In fact, most of Gorer's cases of despair lived alone, and at least a few were pensioners. Gorer also suggested that with these people there had been little or no mourning ritual (funeral ceremonies, wakes, etc.) to stiumlate grief work. Ritual does seem to facilitate grief work (see Rosenblatt, Walsh, & Jackson, 1976, chaps. 4 & 5), but the association of minimal ceremony with social isolation and a slow grief process may mean that people who are relatively isolated lack the social networks and obligations necessary for substantial ceremony, not that minimal ceremony leads to isolation.

Another pathology Gorer reported for the sample he studied was that of not grieving. With those who were not expressing grief, as with those in despair, Gorer extended the theory of grief work beyond individual psychology into sociological and anthropological areas. He found that some people who were not grieving held religious beliefs that minimized the loss involved in a death and stressed minimizing grief expressions. The theory of grief work says quite clearly that no set of beliefs can prevent one from facing situations in which memory or behavioral requirements somehow demand the presence of the deceased and in which the absence of the deceased pushes one to disconnect from the deceased. Nonetheless, the theory of grief work seems to allow for a pattern of behavior and beliefs including limited emotional expression and understandings that minimize some aspects of the loss. A person can, for example, believe that there will be a reunion with the deceased in heaven so that future interaction can be anticipated. That kind of belief might well eliminate the need for some grief work. Grief work may, in a sense, be obstructed by such beliefs, but the disruption may not prevent the bereaved person from arriving at emotionality, personal organization, social life, and work life like those of a person who has had to carry out a full course of grief work while holding a belief that there would never again be contact with the deceased.

Finally, Gorer provided some sense of which losses led to the most difficult and demanding grief work. He thought that the deaths most likely to result in more or less permanent grieving were deaths of adult offspring. Although it is suggested in Chapter 8 that Gorer's finding may apply primarily to situations in which offspring and parent live together, it seems plausible that a death that most disrupts one's plans and one's view of the future would be hardest to deal with. An adult offspring might, for example, be counted on for a sense of continuity of one's line and for emotional and material support. An adult offspring also represents enormous investments of time and energy, so that the loss requires detachment from numerous memories and from the hopes built on the investments.

Theories of the Stages of Grief Work

Stage theories extend the Lindemann and Gorer analyses of grief work, implying that there are distinct places along the route from the grief immediately after the loss to the completed grief work. Stage theories fit easily with the notion of an arrested grieving process, but they imply more. In a simple stage theory, one can define specific points in grief (three, five, ten) and a process that takes one from one stage to the next and is never reversed. Any backsliding or failure to move from one stage to the next would be seen, in such a theory, as a sign of pathology.

Typically stage theories (e.g., Averill, 1968; Bowlby, 1980; De-Vaul, Zisook, & Faschingbauer, 1979; Kubler-Ross, 1969, writing about grief over one's own dying; Pollock, 1961) conceptualize grief as involving an initial stage of denial and/or numbness, followed by a period of acute grief and intense emotion and struggle, followed eventually by some sort of resolution of grief. The stages are, of course, mental constructions of researchers, clinicians, and theoreticians. They are not real, quite abruptly delineable sets of events that are obvious to any observer (cf. Bugen, 1977). Stage concepts seem to go beyond "Mourning and Melancholia" when they are prescriptive. Some stage theories and popularized versions of others make it seem as though there is something wrong with the person whose grief emerges with intensity at some substantial time (say, six months to two years) after the loss (cf. Silver & Wortman, 1980). "Mourning and Melancholia" defines a grief process and an eventual normal outcome, but it does not claim a single unidirectional path for grief work. In fact, it seems not at all inconsistent with the perspective of "Mourning and Melancholia" for normal grief work to involve new surges of grief as one comes upon new memories or hopes that have not yet been detached from the deceased. The likelihood of new surges may be better understood in the context of "reminders," the focus of the next section of this chapter.

Reminder Theory and Grief Work

Another embellishment on the Freudian hypothesis, one linked to theories of learning and performance in psychology, is the notion that specific stimuli set off memories and behavior patterns that are linked to the deceased (Rosenblatt, Walsh, & Jackson, 1976). In this view, what one struggles with during grief work is brought to one's attention by reminders. Grief work is slower if one is out of contact with important reminders, and grief work may not even be necessary for some memories and hopes if one remains out of contact with reminders of them. For example, if a bereaved person remains out of contact with the community in which the bereaved and the deceased had lived, many of the memories of the deceased that are linked to that community would not be recalled. A playground in which deceased and bereaved played together or together watched a child play, a store in which a cherished possession was purchased, a house where the deceased and bereaved shared an unusually tedious or pleasant visit—the number of potential reminders in a specific community may be enormous. Reminders are subjective and would probably be different from person to person. What reminds one person may be a small detail that another would ignore, or a complex arrangement of people, place, weather conditions, and so on that another would not notice. Although this is not the place to develop reminder theory fully, it seems that reminders have varying effects in the grief process. Some reminders may set off memories that are quickly dealt with in the grief process, whereas other reminders or constellations of reminders may have very long-term effects. Reminders of a deceased spouse, for example, may block one from ever remarrying (Rosenblatt, Walsh, & Jackson, 1976, chap. 4).

Even though one may spontaneously recall many memories of the deceased, without reminders there are many others that are unlikely to be recalled for long periods of time or at all. From this perspective, a person can appear to have completed the grief work required by a loss at one point only to hit a period of intense grief when confronted with new reminders (cf. Goin, Burgoyne, & Goin, 1979). Obviously, this view is inconsistent with a unidirectional stage theory which holds that once one has stopped having strong grief feelings those feelings should not or will not recur. Evidence is offered in Chapters 2, 6, 7, 8, and 9, however, for the reminder notion and against the expectation of irreversible progress through stages.

Diaries and Grief Work

A diary may both hinder and facilitate grief work in bereavement. If the process of diary keeping has produced a richer store of memories and hopes, it may lead to more pronounced grieving. If, however, diary keeping focuses attention on a comparatively few memories, hopes, and behavior patterns, the ones recorded in the diary, it may actually facilitate grief work by reducing the number of memories, hopes, and behavior patterns one must disconnect. In addition, diary keeping may help to crystallize one's disconnecting by committing one to what one has put on paper following the loss. On the other hand, the need to write clear thoughts may force one to think about and wrestle with a relatively large number of memories, hopes, and behavioral connections. Furthermore, diary records may give one more stimulus to grief than if one had no records. Thus, it is not clear whether diary keepers have more or less grief work to do than others and are helped or hampered in their grief work by their diary keeping.

4

The Anticipation
of Deaths and Separations

"Monday August 23^d. . . . G. Son Christopher taken Sick this afternoon. . . .

"Saturdy 28. . . . Grand Son Christopher H. Hempstead taken very Sick. . . .

"Mondy 30. . . . the boys about the Same as yesterday except Christ^o who is much poorer. . . .

"Wedy Sept. 1st. . . . Christophers disorder continues to increase and look upon him dangerous.

"Thursdy 2^d. . . . Grand son Christopher H. Hempst^d continues very low, distressed in his Stomac and Baffled all medical aid and about the Seting of the Sun he died."

Diary of Stephen Hempstead, Sr. Excerpts for August and September, 1819. (Hempstead, 1958, pp. 282-283, ad passim).

* * *

"August 21, 1897. Baby sick today. . . .

"August 22, 1897. . . . Baby is sick yet, poor little darling. Oh what a mother must go through. . . .

"August 24, 1897. . . . Jacob is sick today too. Hope he will get well soon. It is so hard to see little babies sick. . . .

"August 25, 1897. Baby awful sick this morning. We went to the city to get a Dr. We are waiting for the Dr. now. Ole has been home six hours. Oh my poor little darling Jacob looks like he's going to leave us. My, why don't that Dr. come. I have got the headache but that is nothing only my baby was well.

"Evening, August 25, 1897. Jacob is dead. Tears blind my eyes as I write. Oh my how sick he was, but now he is at rest, my little darling Jacob. Hope to meet you in heaven. God help me to bear my sorrow. Oh, we do not know when our time has come, when death cometh with his cold hand and taketh us away.

Birget is here tonight. She dressed my little Jacob for the last time. <u>May peace be with his dust and blessed be his memory</u>."

Diary of Sophia Lovick, unpublished manuscript loaned by Rosalie Norem, Ames, Iowa. Some spelling and punctuation converted to standard usage. Underscored material translated from Norwegian by Josephine Haugan and Per Lund.

* * *

February 16, 1810. "Less hope than ever. The Dr. no longer speaks encouraging, but fears the lamp of life is nearly exhausted, with what agonizing distress, <u>void of hope</u> do I now watch the distressed countenance of my Dear Hartley, a countenance that once beamed <u>pleasure, gayety, & health</u>—now the scourges of pain & sickness have strongly marked each linament with sorrow."

February 18, 1810. "The most wretched day of my life as yet, but Oh, it only leads me to expect one far more so. . . ."

March 4, 1810. "The trial is past & yet I live. . . ."

Diary of Sophia Sewell Wood, unpublished manuscript, Manuscripts and Archives Division, Sterling Memorial Library, Yale University.

* * * * * * *

Anticipatory grief may be defined as grief that starts before a loss has actually occurred and that results from an expectation of the loss. According to one version of the theory of grief work (see Chapter 3) one comes to terms with a loss, detaches oneself from a person lost through death or permanent separation, and disconnects one's memories, hopes, mental associations, habits, and so on from the person. Only then, according to the theory, can one be rid of grief and function fully. If some of the grief work can occur before the actual fact of loss or separation, the theory might predict an earlier termination of grief after the loss (Fulton & Gottesman, 1980). The present chapter probes the implications of that view of anticipatory grief and raises questions about the nature of anticipation and expectation when someone close to one may soon be lost through separation or death.

In the passages just quoted from the Hempstead, Lovick, and Wood diaries, the diarists gave some sense of anticipating a loss. But neither Hempstead nor Lovick seemed convinced, until the day the loss actually occurred, that it was likely. Did Hempstead, Lovick, or Wood begin to grieve for the loss before it actually occurred? It is difficult to decide. And it is difficult to decide if anticipatory grief, even when it was clearly there, as it was in the passage from the Wood diary, is like grief after the loss. Sophia Sewell Wood, four months after the death of her own husband, wrote about a friend whose husband was dying, "Oh, poor Mary I can feel for you. You know not yet, you cannot realize half you are to suffer." (Diary of Sophia Sewell Wood, unpublished manuscript, Manuscripts and Archives Division, Sterling Memorial Library, Yale University, entry of July 10, 1810). Wood may have been saying that from her perspective, that of a 21-year-old widow, one cannot anticipate the feelings and experiences of loss.

What Goes on during the Anticipatory Period?

If things that go on in the anticipation process—for example, saying goodbye to the lost, thinking through how one will live after the loss, and grieving—have effects after the loss, one would need data on whether those things went on or not, but the diarists in the first two passages cited at the beginning of this chapter gave no clues, and Wood wrote only of grieving. The diary data may be inadequate for studying anticipatory grief, but studies of anticipatory grief among twentieth-century North Americans are also deficient in such data. At this point, one can only assume that grieving, emotional detaching, and cognitive disconnecting go on when a person anticipates a loss. In the long run, of course, there will be investigations of the assumed processes. Those investigations will have to explore the thoughts and feelings of the prospective bereaved person and his or her interaction with the dying person. Case reports and theoretical discussions often indicate the importance of social interactions before loss (e.g. Gut, 1974), and there are indications that these interactions can have an impact on subsequent grief (Carey, 1977). But as of this writing there seems to be no study that traces thoughts, interactions, and feelings in the anticipatory period and then assesses reactions following the loss. There are literary examples (Bertman, 1980), but apparently no empirical studies. Until these aspects of the anticipatory process are assessed, studies will lump together people who actually anticipated a loss and people who did not, people who planned ahead and people who did not, people who made a kind of peace with the person who was eventually lost and people who did not.

Hope is another important factor in understanding the effects of anticipating a loss. Hope for recovery seems common when people are ill, even fatally ill, with little chance for recovery. In the following two sets of excerpts, hope punctuated concern over serious illnesses that ended in death.

* * * * * * *

"Received news this morning that my dear brother John is dangerously sick. . . . Found him suffering under an attack of gout, which for the first time seemed to have reached the brain. . . ."—entry of December 4, 1863.

". . . brother John was a little better yesterday morning, still in a critical state."—entry of December 6.

". . . Went to bed greatly comforted [by a conversation with the doctor] hoping to find my dear patient better in the morning."—entry of December 11.

"This morning about 7, George, who watched with his uncle all night, came up & said that he breathed much shorter and that phlegm was collecting. . . . I hastened down & found him greatly distressed for breath. . . . While I was up there [shaving] my dear, dear brother, breathed his last! I was not called, because the family supposed that I had not returned from the post office. When I came out of my room, I was thunderstruck with the announcement that he had been dead ten minutes. His reason held out, I think, to the last. He said his agony was terrible. Mary repeated to him 'The Lord is my Shepherd . . .' and she thought he replied, 'repeat more. . . .' Thus has passed away my precious, precious brother John. Oh how can I bear it? Lord Jesus support me under this crushing blow! . . .—entry of December 12.

Diary of Elisha Lord Cleaveland, a New Haven minister, unpublished manuscript from Manuscripts and Archives Division, Sterling Memorial Library, Yale University.

* * *

On November 4, 1845, George H. Durrie, a 25-year-old artist, reported in his diary that his brother-in-law, John Smith, was dying. Subsequent references to John Smith and to dying were as follows:

"Feel very sad indeed this eve. Can realize fully the shortness of life. Oh! what a great thing it is to die. May we *ever* be prepared."—entry of November 5.

". . . We have some hope of his getting better. . . ."—entry of November 6.

". . . John begins to bleed. . . ."—entry of November 7.

". . . [John] kept growing worse every day. . . . He sunk gradually till he *died*, which was on Sunday morning at about 10 o'clk, Nov. 16th. Father went out there in the morning and saw him die. Austin came in at noon and brought the news. Oh! what sorrow burst in upon us at the melancholy news of his death. He, who four weeks before was well among us is now *dead!* Sarah went down to Father's this afternoon. . . . Have had a bad headache all day. Have not been to church. . . . What an afflicted family. All is sorrow and weeping."—entry of Sunday, November 16.

Diary of George H. Durrie. Unpublished transcript, Manuscripts and Archives Division, Sterling Memorial Library, Yale University.

* * * * * * *

In both of these cases there were moments of hope. Did the hope reduce the effects of psychological preparation for the death or even prevent such preparation? Was the hope really hope, or was it an expression of good wishes or loyalty? The diary data are not rich enough to allow a formal study of hope. It seems clear, however, that hope is among the phenomena that may occur during a period of anticipating a loss and that must be looked at in order to understand the anticipation process. Anticipatory grief studies that focus on situations of almost certain, predictable death, such as chronic childhood leukemia (e.g., Futterman, Hoffman, & Sabshin, 1972), may be the only studies in which the anticipatory "grief process" is like that following a death. But even then anticipatory grief may be blended with hope (Bluebond-Langner, 1977, p. 205). For the typical case of apparent dying, in which signs sometimes point to improvement or recovery, the anticipation process may be quite different.

Perhaps most often people do not really grieve in advance of a loss in the way that they do following a loss (Clayton, Desmarais, & Winokur, 1968; Parkes, 1970; Pine, 1974; Silverman, 1974). Other words than "grief" may be needed—worrying, despairing while hoping for the best, grasping for straws, fantasizing potential outcomes, trying not to think about the worst that can happen. Some studies seem to find that longer anticipation reduces at least some aspects or symptoms of post-loss grieving (e.g., Ball, 1977; Glick, Weiss, & Parkes, 1974; Parkes, 1972 [Boston data but not London data], 1975a, 1975b). But in these studies, people anticipating death for longer periods may have been led to expect losses with more certainty because of the pronouncements of physicians and their own inclinations to believe them. In modern times, the course of some diseases, particularly of some cancers, is relatively predictable. And some physicians are inclined or are pushed by patients and patients' relatives to make precise predictions. Thus, some people nowadays may, well in advance of a death, definitely expect the death to occur within a specified time. However, Parkes has also established, on a sample of London widows, that many people are at first disinclined to believe a fatal prognosis (Parkes, 1972, p. 83).

Although some researchers have attempted to use retrospective accounts to explore hope and anticipatory processes, it is too easy for respondents to forget or to distort because of the dynamics of the subsequent grief process. Even the fact of having anticipated a death is difficult to establish retrospectively. As Fischhoff (1975, 1977, 1980) has demonstrated, people are inclined in retrospect to see more orderliness in past events than they did at the time and to claim more certainty in anticipating events than they actually had. Moreover, straightforward questions about something like "hope," even if asked during the anticipatory period, may be of little use because people may be reluctant to confess that they have given up hope or that they have hope for cure of a disease defined as incurable. In addition, asking people whether they are still hoping for another's recovery may push them to do such hoping. They may feel it would be disloyal not to hope, and to confess that hope no longer exists may be too appalling to acknowledge to self or to others.

It would have been valuable to have diary rich in information on the anticipation process, enabling the exploration of factors like hope and to differentiate among people whose anticipation was realistic and consistent and those whose anticipation was not. But the diary data scarcely ever contain that kind of information. The quotes given in this chapter from the Hempstead, Lovick, Wood, Cleaveland, and Durrie diaries are characteristic of anticipation data from the diaries. Details of thought and feeling seem never to have been entered by diarists recording that someone might be dying.

Producing firm estimations of duration of anticipation of death was even a problem; people rarely said (or perhaps believed) that death would certainly (1) occur within some specified time that was less than the normal life span of the ill person and (2) be due to a disease already present. However, the diary data are extended in the tabulations of this study over three years following the loss. Such over-time data with a fine grain of measurement (daily in some cases) are unduplicated in published research to date, yet as Pine (1974) has asserted, studies of anticipatory grief without grief data over time may be of little use. In addition, the data of the present study are largely contemporaneous, not retrospective. If people systematically distort memories of their grief, the diary data provide a more sensitive test of the relation of possible variations in anticipation of loss to grief following the loss. Thus, the diary data may be relatively free of some of the artifacts that have operated in previous studies.

If the "work" of grief begins when one suspects a loss is going to occur, the theory of grief work might lead to the prediction that the greater the number of days of anticipation, the less would be the grief after the loss. Some of the grief work would have been done before the loss. However, long-term anticipation may appear at times to lead to less grief because the emotional exhaustion following the prolonged terminal illness of somebody important to one may lead to temporary numbness, to a temporary suppression of grief work following a loss, or even to relief that a long and excruciating struggle is over. Anticipation may even lead to enhancement of grief—for example, if long-term anticipation increases one's involvement in the care of the dying person and if that care makes the loss, when it occurs, hurt more or leaves one with more memories and emotional involvement to disengage from the lost. That may have been one factor responsible for the finding by Gerber, Rusalem, Hannon, Battin, and Arkin (1975) that is a sample of older widows and widowers, the 77% who anticipated a loss for more than six months subsequently showed more signs of illness. The effect of long-term care, visiting, and concern may have made the loss more stressful than a sudden loss would have been. Thus, a case can be made for greater anticipation being associated with less grief after a loss or, in contrast to what might be derived from the theory of grief work, for greater anticipation being associated with greater grief.

"Anticipation" and Grief in the Diary Data

For many losses experienced by the diarists, it was possible to estimate the number of days of "anticipating" (which was defined for this study as "knowing or suspecting") that a loss was to occur. The number of days might be determined by the first day of very high fever or convulsions in a child, the first day a physician diagnosed an untreatable cancer, or the first day the diarist reported that emigration or a long trip was planned. There were, however, instances of anticipating a loss in which the loss did not occur. A very sick child recovered; a planned trip was called off.

In some cases what appears to be the anticipation of a loss might at least in part be defensive. A diarist may, for example, have written as though a sick child would die, while not actually believing the loss would occur. The diarist may have been either guarding against great shock if the child should die or avoiding a challenge to God or to fate. In many cases anticipation had to be inferred from statements such as Hempstead's and Lovick's quoted above, although the diarist never said anything explicit about anticipating a death or separation or said it only very shortly before the loss. For the five cases of anticipation of loss quoted so far in this chapter, the estimated number of days of anticipation are: Hempstead, 12; Lovick, 4; Wood, not determinable; Cleaveland, 8; Durrie, 13.

For the average death recorded in the diaries for which the days of anticipating loss could be estimated, the mean is 56 days of anticipation, with a standard deviation of 171 days. For separations, the mean number of days of anticipation is 41, with a standard deviation of 84 days.

Although one might think that the onset of anticipating a separation would be quite straightforward, it was much more difficult to estimate the number of days of anticipating a separation than of a death. The estimation could be made for only 55 of 176 separations (31%), while it could be made for 114 of 142 deaths (80%). The difference may say something about the relative significance of pending separations and pending deaths in people's lives or the relative demands on people's time of a dying person as opposed to a person from whom one is going to be separated. Forthcoming deaths received much more coverage in diaries than forthcoming separations. At any rate, the fact that the number of days of anticipation could not even be estimated for 149 losses may suggest that the estimations that were made were not made with excessive recklessness.

The data were coded so that the greatest number of days of anticipation possible was 999. This limitation, which applied to only two cases of loss, represents a suspicion that anticipation longer than that length of time loses its psychological impact, if there is any psychological impact from anticipation. Parkes made a similar choice, in his analysis of anticipatory grief data (1975a, pp. 132-133), when he chose to count abrupt terminations of long illnesses as short-term anticipations. The diary data give some scattered hints that for the diarists a death after a long illness may have been as unexpected as a sudden death. Consider the following passage from the diary of Harry Croswell.

* * * * * * *

"While at dinner opened the Argus and found an account of the death of my brother, Dr. Thos. O'H. Croswell of Catskill. He was my oldest brother, 77 years old, and always been a kind brother to me. Though he has long been infirm, the intelligence was wholly unexpected, having rec[d] no letter until a few hours afterwards. . . ." Diary of Harry Croswell, unpublished manuscript, Manuscript and Archives Division, Sterling Memorial Library, Yale University, entry of January 19, 1844.

* * * * * * *

Statistical analyses are presented in greater detail in Appendix C. The statistical trends are weak but consistent. With longer anticipation of a separation there tended to be less grief.

It may be that anticipation of a separation leads to anticipatory grief work, but it may also be that such anticipation leads to interaction that somehow mutes the actual loss. One may, for example, make clearer plans to correspond with the person to be lost, made a firmer commitment for reunion, or develop shared understandings of the separation that might minimize some of the grief-producing elements in a separation (felt rejection, loss of opportunity to discuss the past, unfinished but finishable interpersonal business). Though it is very difficult to measure aspects of interaction during the pre-separation period, the diary data provide some intriguing anecdotes. Consider the following excerpt from the 1863 diary of a convalescing Civil War soldier who was soon to leave his wife and return to the battlefront.

* * * * * * *

"October 4, Sunday morning. Another month has slipped by, and my leave will be over soon. . . .

"October 25, Sunday evening. Only fourteen days are left to the hour when I shall have to be in Dixie. I shall be two days on the road. . . .

"November 3, Tuesday afternoon. In a little time I shall be again in Dixie. I have enjoyed a very happy and fairly long time. I have learned to value this love, which, although it was so strong as to dispose me to unite myself forever with the angel who gives it to me, yet appears to increase from day to day. . . .

"November 4, Wednesday evening. . . . It made me very sad when I could not be with my darling every moment on the eve of my departure for the war. The least thing made us burst into tears. Sarah and the old folks came back this evening. I am very sorry for that, because I love so much to be alone and happy with my sweet wife.

"November 5, Thursday evening. The last day of my stay here has gone. Tomorrow morning I must leave. . . . My sweet wife and I went for a walk today, and finished the life of H. Greeley. We love one another, and dread parting.

"November 6, Friday morning. The dreaded day has finally come. I write with a trembling hand. I have just enjoyed a sweet, glorious, sublime season with my darling, my beautiful, the life of my heart, my existence. Without her I should not wish to live longer. I am going to leave this morning all that makes me happy, the woman for whom I live. What cruelty! Shall I ever see her again? I shall always hope. . . ."

Excerpts from *Young Ward's Diary* (1935, pp. 122-125, ad passim). Ward survived the war.

* * * * * * *

These excerpts from Ward's diary support the notion (to the extent that an illustration can support a general case) that long-term anticipation (50 days in Ward's case, whereas the median for all separations is 10.75 days) is associated with commitment to the relationship and interaction that may minimize felt rejection.

For deaths the data are rather different. Again, the statistical details are given in greater detail in Appendix C. For all deaths taken together, there is no relationship between length of anticipation of a death and subsequent grief. However, when diarists were not living with the deceased, anticipation tended to be associated with less grief in the first two years of loss. Apparently, grief work is facilitated by anticipation of a death when one is able to disconnect from the dying person, which is the case when one is not living with that person. The diary data suggest that one can, during the anticipation period, disconnect from memories, ideas, and behavior patterns if one is not living with a dying person.

The finding that coresidence has an effect on anticipatory grief suggests that home care for the dying, which was quite common in the nineteenth century and which is discussed further in the next chapter, may have made anticipatory grief work difficult. For people living with the dying, anticipatory grief work may not occur, or if it occurs, it may be offset by the acquisition of additional memories, ideas, and behavior links that need to be worked on following the death. Even if one has done some anticipatory grief work, after long hope (or uncertainty) and struggle in support of that hope (or uncertainty), one's efforts may seem to be invalidated by the death, which may increase grief. Moreover, a daily routine that centers on nursing the sick person would be ended by the death, and a new pattern would have to be developed. Such a change in routine and role may augment grief. A diarist typically would have continued to live amid reminders of the life pattern that involved so much nursing and suffering, and that may further have increased the difficulty of coming to terms with the death.

The comparison between reactions to the death of a household member and to the death of someone living elsewhere is not a simple one to interpret. With coresidence there was, on the average, a longer period of anticipation of loss; and, of course, one is more likely to be dependent on a coresident. It would be useful to evaluate more directly the involvement of the diarists in the care of coresidents who were ill, but that cannot be done. Although there are diaries with substantial detail about such involvement (see the next chapter, for examples), diarists who lived with a terminally ill relative and who said little or nothing about involvement in care are a puzzle. Were they not involved in care? Was care typically not needed? Were they involved in care but not reporting it in the diary? The diary data are unhelpful because it is impossible to know who among diarists coresident with somebody terminally ill was uninvolved in terminal care. But the data suggest that when survivor and decedent were not coresident and, hence, the survivor had no involvement in care of the dying, the longer the period of anticipation of loss the less the grief, at least in the first year or bereavement.

Summary and Conclusions

Although the diary data on anticipatory grief have some of the same defects as data in other studies on the subject, the diary data have the twin advantages of giving repeated measures over a period of years and of giving contemporaneous rather than retrospective accounts. In the diary data, longer anticipation of separation is to a modest extent associated with less grief. Although this effect may be due to anticipatory grieving, a case can be made for the effect being the result of interactions that reduce some of the grieving elements of separation. Longer anticipations may be associated with a greater commitment for reunion, clearer plans to maintain communication during the separation, and the finishing of finishable interpersonal business.

For deaths too, longer anticipation is associated with less grief, but only if diarist and decedent were not coresident. For diarists coresident with the decedent, even though long anticipation may enable some grief work, longer anticipation was associated in the nineteenth century with greater involvement in care of the dying and with uncertainty about prognosis. When a long period of struggle, uncertainty, and hope is ended, it may take much longer to recover from the loss. This interpretation, however, may not be generalizable to contemporary situations in which (1) medical knowledge enables a sure prediction of death within some time period from a disease whose process is already evident, and (2) the terminally ill are nursed outside the home. In contemporary situations there may often be anticipatory grieving undiluted by hope, and reduced involvement in the long-term care of a close relative may reduce the psychological devastation felt when death occurs. One often does not lose the heavily involving role of caretaker or nurse, and living apart from the dying person during terminal illness may, after the death, both reduce the grief impact of stimuli in the dwelling and increase one's capacity to function in that setting. The "kindness of strangers" (Bertman, 1980) in caring for the terminally ill may be a kindness not only to the dying person but to those kin and friends who would otherwise participate in daily care.

5

Health, Medical Care, and Grief

The discussion in Chapter 4 of anticipatory grief raised the possibility that medical beliefs and practices have an effect on the grief process. Since the establishment of a predictable time course for some fatal illnesses is a recent phenomenon, the anticipatory grief that might come with certain expectation of death may, as a consequence, also be of recent origin. The present chapter explores predictability further through probing possible relationships of grief to the high child and maternal death rates of the nineteenth century. I also speculated in Chapter 4 that involvement in medical care may have an impact on grief. The present chapter documents the heavy involvement of the diarists in providing medical care and their heavy contact with dying and death, and explores the relationship of that involvement and contact to various aspects of grief.

Deaths of Infants and Young Children

In its most simple version (see Chapter 4), an anticipatory-grief version of the theory of grief work would suggest that expecting a loss may lead to lessened grief. If one expects a loss, one may be better prepared, may have already thought through some of the adjustments that have to be made, and may have either begun disengaging or have all along withheld engaging from the person who is likely to die.

The death rate throughout the nineteenth century was high for infants and young children. Statistics cannot be provided for the diary sample on the death rate for infants and young children in the families or communities of the diarists. But the proportion of deaths of children age two or younger reported in the diaries was much higher at the beginning of the century than later. As Table 5.1 indicates, the death rate for children age two or less dropped in the diary reports over the course of the century. That 12 of the 78 deaths (15%) for which there were age data were of infants and young children suggests a far higher death rate for this age group than is true for the latter part of the twentieth century in North America. Less than 7% of all deaths in the United States in 1970 were of children age newborn through 14 years (United States Bureau of the Census, 1975, p. 60). This is not to say that it was normal for a nineteenth-century infant or young child to die. Far more newborns grew to adulthood than died in infancy or childhood, even in the early part of the century.

Table 5.1. Death in the Sample by Quartile of the Nineteenth Century

	Persons Age 2 or Younger	Persons Age 3 or Older	Percentage of Deaths in the Younger Group
1801-1825	2	10	17
1826-1850	4	16	20
1851-1875	5	28	15
1876-1900	1	12	8

Note: These data are only for cases in which the precise age of the deceased is known.

An indirect indication of the cause of death for infants and young children can be found in the diary data on when infants and young children died. Ten of the 12 deaths of children age two or younger recorded in the diaries (83%) occurred during the warm months of May through September. By contrast, the deaths of all other people were distributed exactly as one would expect by chance, 42% in the five warm months and 58% in the seven cooler months. Diarrheal diseases, intestinal parasites, and malaria, all of which might particularly threaten young children, were more common or more serious in warm months.

The high U.S. birth rate in the early part of the nineteenth century (Grabill, Kiser, & Whelpton, 1958) may have been in part a result of the high death rate for infants and young children. People who had lost a child might have had another, which they would otherwise not have had, to replace it. A new child in a diarist's family occasionally was given the same name as a dead child—a sign, perhaps, that the new baby was seen as a replacement. However, no diarist wrote as though a child was a replacement for another, and the use of the name of a deceased child for a new child might be merely an indication that it was important that someone carry the name, perhaps in honor of a relative.

People who thought they might eventually lose some children might have had more children than they otherwise would have had, in part as insurance against the loss. The insurance might have been expecially important because the families of the diarists in the sample seemed to value help provided by children. Elkanah Walker, for example, reported with apparent pride and pleasure that his eight-year-old son Cyrus helped herd the cattle, hoe potatoes, and kill magpies that were pests in the family granary (E. Walker, 1976, pp. 395, 406, 408).

Some of the diarists seemed to see grown children as insurance against a destitute or infirm old age or to be seen that way by their own parents or parents-in-law. William Brisbane was one of several diarists in the sample who gave a grown offspring assets in exchange for assistance in old age.

* * * * * * *

"Wife having desired it I agreed to let our son William & his family take our house & the farm & have her & myself to board with them for the rent thereof, & he is also to keep my riding horse for me, find us in wood & light, pay the insurance & taxes. . . . It is not by any means my preference to live so, but I do it entirely to gratify my dear old wife. . . ."

Diary of William H. Brisbane, unpublished manuscript, State Historical Society of Wisconsin, entry of September 25, 1875.

* * * * * * *

However, the arrangement was terminated as a result of relationship tensions: "William has concluded on account of the difficulty of his wife and mother to get along together to give up the house &

farm & to go at something else" (William H. Brisbane diary, entry of April 11, 1876).

Two years later, after William H. Brisbane had died, his elderly widow was living with their daughter. Again there were relationship difficulties.

* * * * * * *

"Mother treats me . . . as if I were a child and did not know how to do anything much without being told, although I own the house & most of the things in it & have the care of the housekeeping, yet she does & talks as [though] every thing belonged to her, lending or giving away my things without so much as consulting me at all. . . ."

Diary of P. Adeline Brisbane, unpublished manuscript, State Historical Society of Wisconsin, Madison, entry of March 25, 1878.

* * * * * * *

The problems the Brisbanes had with providing room and board to the family elders suggest that it may be a bit too romantic to imagine that family life was improved when elderly people who needed help lived with grown offspring. Nonetheless, in the world of the diarists, care in old age was an important gain that might be realized from one's offspring (cf. Rosenblatt, Peterson, Portner, et al, 1973, dealing with a worldwide sample). The motivation for having children was, then, substantial. However, no diarist wrote of having many children as a way of insuring that there would be "enough" children.

This discussion of reasons for having children assumes that people had some control over the production of children, that they could have chosen to have fewer children, and that they were more likely to do so as the century progressed because they could be assured of having more children survive. Does a high birth rate reflect valuing or disvaluing of children? Was birth control even an option for the diarists? William H. Brisbane, the one diarist who was a physician, reported fitting pessaries (cervical caps) by 1870. No other diarist mentioned birth control. In several diaries, however, there were indications that spouses were temporarily sleeping apart and avoiding intercourse because one was angry with the other. And several other diarists were separated from a spouse for long periods because of the husband's participation in the California gold rush or the Civil War, his search for new land to farm, or the wife's visit to distant relatives. There was never a suggestion that these separations were defined as pregnancy limitation, although that may have been in people's awareness and even a reason for some of the separations. With the exception of Lester Ward, who wrote about his premarital sexual adventures, and several diarists who gossiped about other people's sex lives, no diarist wrote about sex. Despite knowledge of what can be assumed to be people's most private records, it is impossible to know what, if anything, they tried to do to limit births. Apparently sexuality was too dangerous (Faragher, 1979, p. 147) or too personal to write about even in a private record. Nonetheless, there is evidence in other studies that by the middle of the nineteenth century women were seeking and at times finding contraception and abortion (Sklar, 1973, p. 208), and it seems that even long before the nineteenth century people were effectively limiting the number of children they had through coitus interruptus or reservatus, abortion, and perhaps infanticide (Wrigley, 1972).

The fact that many women in the world of the diarists died in childbirth or as a result of complications following childbirth (see the next section of this chapter) would certainly have been a strong reason to delay pregnancies and to limit their number, and so would have been the economic problems of supporting many young children. Another reason was simply the burden of dealing with a large number of children. Mary White wrote, as did several other women diarists in the sample, of a need for temporary liberation from the burden of a large brood of children: "How much do I this day long for some hiding place from the busy cares and interruptions of a large family" (diary of Mary White, unpublished manuscript, Huntington Library, entry of August 31, 1841). Even one child could be too much.

* * * * * * *

"I have been obliged to give up writing in my journal every day, my crying baby takes up too much of my time. . . . Sometimes it seems as if I should be crazy."

Diary of Mrs. Charles C. Carpenter, unpublished filmed copy, Public Archives of Canada, Ottawa, entry of December 15, 1863.

* * * * * * *

If the birth rate in the early part of the century was related to the high death rate for young children, one might reason that children were valued less as individuals in the early part of the century. In fact, it is often asserted, in part on the basis of birth or death rate data, that children are less valued as individuals when people have, or lose, more children (cf. Stannard, 1974, 1977, pp. 58-61, writing about parents and children in Puritan New England). But the clinical literature seems to say that child deaths increase the intensity with which parents invest in surviving children (Krell & Rabkin, 1979).

And the diary data seem inconsistent with the idea that high death rates lead to less parental valuing of young children. The idea that young children were valued less when their death rate was comparatively high implies that the earlier in the nineteenth century a child died the less would be parental grief. When the diary data are examined, the reverse seems to be the case. For the 12 deaths of children two years of age or younger, the earlier in the century the greater the grief. To be specific, for nine of the first 36 months of bereavement there is variability in grief over the death of a child age two or less; for the other months grief is the same in all cases—there is none. In all nine months of bereavement with data variability, the earlier in the century the child died the greater was parental grief. The data are not overwhelmingly strong, but they certainly do not support the notion that young children were devalued earlier in the century, when they were less likely to survive.

As the excerpts from the Lovick diary in Chapters 4 and 9, the Squire diary in Chapter 9, and the Huntington diary quoted immediately below suggest, the loss of a young child could be quite a heavy blow to people living in the nineteenth century.

* * * * * * *

"This year is nearly closed, & it has been an eventful year to me. In the course of it, one of the tenderest ties by wh. I was connected with *any* creature has been sundered. My Joshua was smitten, & my heart bleeds still. It was a bitter cup, but God showed me that I merited it, & kept me from rebelling, blessed be His name, so that I gave up what he so suddenly demanded without disputing His right so to do. It was a heavy trial tho' not to be compared with the death of my husband. *Then* my faculties seemed stunned. I look back & perfectly remember my feelings, & am sure that for six or eight months after that event my faculties all seemed by the blow shook from their proper balance. It was a different sort of life from anything I ever experienced. Afflicted as much as my nature cd bear on the one hand, & comforted & stayed up by the Omnipotent arm on the other, my intense exercises overpowered my poor frame, & I was 'like those who dream'. But my sweet Joshua's death affects me with an inexpressible *tenderness.* Oh that its effects may be *lasting.* Beloved of my soul! Dear cherished, lamented child! May thy removal rouse up thy mother to more persevering & unwavering diligence in finishing her work. May we all meet in Heaven."

Diary of Susan Mansfield Huntington, unpublished manuscript, Manuscripts and Archives Division, Sterling Memorial Library, Yale University, entry of December 23, 1821. Joshua died about September 12, 1821, at age two.

* * * * * * *

Why did Huntington mourn her lost Joshua in this year-end review? Possibly Joshua was unusually important because he was born after the death of Huntington's husband; Joshua might, for example, have helped in all the ways a needy and developing child can help, to blunt Huntington's grief for her dead husband. But it may be that the child was special only in a way that babies and youngest children typically were during the nineteenth century. The feeding, touching, comforting, and carrying of a baby, and cleaning its soiled clothing, may have been sufficient to bond care-taker to child quite strongly. The ordinary social development of a child, the smiling at and clinging to familiar people, might also produce a strong parent-child tie.

For much of the nineteenth century there were few occupations open to the majority of women except that of housewife and mother (Douglas, 1977, pp. 55-64). Mothering might thus have been more important for women at that time than it is now. Women had rela-tively few alternative outlets for relationships and for their creative energy. A baby, as the most recent and most dependent addition to the family, may have received an unusual amount of attention, much more than a previous child would, particularly from a mother. It is clear that some of the diarists were fascinated by their young chil-dren. Perhaps more women than men were, although some men clearly were. The fascination is reflected in detailed reports, in some of the diaries, of the physical and intellectual development of a child, quotes of interesting things the child said, and descriptions of some of the child's accomplishments and expressions of strong emotion. It may have been rare and next to impossible for a parent, especially a mother who had more contact with infants and young children and more responsibility for their care, to distance an infant (cf. Cott, 1977, p. 144). Moreover, the risks of death, the pain, and other trials of pregnancy and childbirth may have led to great valuing of children, particularly by women. To have risked and invested so much could not be easily justified if one failed to value the product of that risk and investment.

Huntington's comparison of the loss of a child with the loss of a husband is not relevant to the question of whether people devalue young children if they are relatively likely to die. The relationship of spouses is different in so many ways from the relationship of parent and child that it would not be surprising to find that grief is, in the long run, much more intense for a spouse than for a young child (which it in fact is in the diary data). The relevant comparison for understanding whether children have been devalued at some point in time is a comparison across historical periods of reactions to children and to the loss of children.

What makes some scholars think that children were less valued than they seem in the diary data to have been? One fact sometimes cited is that there was at times a delay in the naming of children (Saum, 1974). Although a delay may indicate that people were less attached to a child than if the child had been named, the delay may mean other things. Christening may have awaited the arrival of a minister, the preparation of christening clothes, or parental inspiration about names. A name may not have been perceived as necessary until a child was old enough to respond to it. Moreover, the label attached to an infant ("baby," "wee one") before it was named may have been as meaningful and emotion-charged as any name.

Another kind of evidence cited at times in support of the notion that children were undervalued is the frequency of admonitions in letters, sermons, and the like not to invest oneself too heavily in a child who cannot be counted on to live (Saum, 1974). However, that too has multiple interpretations. The fact that people needed to be admonished suggests that they were making such investments (cf. Ilick, 1974, writing about the seventeenth century). And the meaning of the admonition may be something other than a warning to invest less. It may, for example, have been a religious instruction, saying that one should worship no other God but the one God. Some people may have believed that too strong an investment in a child may so offend God that God would take the child's life. Alternatively, as the following excerpts from the diaries of Sally Squire and Mary White suggest, a major issue that may have been reflected in admonitions not too invest oneself in a child was whether, despite great grief, one could still accept whatever happened as God's will.

* * * * * * *

"Have now returned from the house of mourning! . . . This is a very affecting scene; especially to the Parents—to see their tender offspring laid in the cold Earth—may they not repine . . . but bless God's holy name. . . . Perhaps this Child was like to come too much between them and their God. . . ."

Diary of Sally Squire, unpublished manuscript, New York Public Library, entry of November 9, 1815.

* * *

"My Heavenly Father has been in different ways teaching me that this is not my house. . . . I have not heeded his warnings as I ought to have done. First he took my dear little Norman & laid me upon a bed of suffering for many months. He then sent whooping cough into my family & while some of the children had it lightly others were so severely ill as to cause us much solicitude. But my heart was not filled with gratitude as it should have been that they were all spared & now he has come & smitten down our healthiest & one of our loveliest ones. Oh that he would teach me the meaning of all this & help me so to profit by it that he will not need to send upon me a heavier chastisement. . . ."

Diary of Mary White, unpublished manuscript, Huntington Library, entry of July 2, 1842.

* * * * * * *

Counseling people to be prepared for a possible loss may represent realistic awareness of death rates, but the consequence of that awareness may be something other than emotional distance. Recognizing the possibility of loss one may think through to some extent how one would live if the loss occurred, but that does not necessarily mean that one distances the person one might lose. It is doubtful, to take a contemporary example, that the purchase of life insurance, which represents an acknowledgment of possible loss, leads to emotional detachment of prospective beneficiary from the insured. When a new parent was counseled to "in some degree turn . . . affections away from" a new baby (Saum, 1974, p. 486) that may not have meant that the baby received any less love and attention than a twentieth-century North American baby receives. People may even love more the child they fear they will lose. It seems neither obvious nor proved that infants and young children were devalued in the nineteenth century. Perhaps mothers were more attached to them than were fathers, though in the diary data there are not sufficient cases to make a comparison of maternal and paternal reactions to the deaths of infants and young children productive. But the normal contact that people, particularly mothers, would have had to maintain with an infant seems sufficient to attach a person quite strongly to the youngster.

Maternal Deaths

The same argument that was made about expectations and the deaths of infants and young children can be made about expectations and the death of women in childbirth. If people expected such deaths, might they be better prepared to deal with the loss? The death of women in childbirth might provide a stronger test of hypotheses about expectations or anticipatory grief, since a diarist's involvements with an adult might be greater and more complex. A person might have a stronger sense of how horrible a loss of a closely related adult would be and hence work harder, given the expectation of a substantial likelihood of death, at being prepared for the loss.

Death in childbearing was common in the nineteenth century, particularly in the early part of the century. Although most pregnancies did not end in the woman's death, people did not view childbearing with the optimism that is so common in the twentieth century. Women frequently looked forward with genuine fear to delivering a child. Consider, for example, the following quotes from the diaries of Linka Keyser, Susan Mansfield Huntington, Mary White, and Mrs. Charles C. Carpenter.

* * * * * * *

". . . In a couple of months I shall again become a mother. It is, indeed, painful and hard; but God's will be done!—Hexa [diarist's sister], thy death was the result of bearing a child; Mother's death also; I cannot know what God may have ordained for me; but His will be done; may we all, as Death calls us, be prepared."

Diary of Linka Keyser (1952, p. 256), entry of June 30, 1854.

* * *

"My nerves are all unstrung. I am afraid that if I live I shall be no comfort to any body, & I don't feel that exercises of faith wh. makes me willing to die. Oh I am in a state of great distress. . . . Mrs. Farrer has engaged to take Susan in case of my death. Mother Jabez, Joseph; sister Betsey will take Sarah. Mrs. Cutler or Armstrong dear little Mary, & I think sister Sally in Killingworth my poor Elizabeth." Entry of November 27, 1819.

"Have never been in so much distress as now . . . expecting every hour I may be confined. . . . Fear for my future reason. Oh god, have mercy, have mercy. . . ." Entry of November 30, 1819.

Diary of Susan Mansfield Huntington, unpublished manuscript, Manuscripts and Archives Division, Sterling Memorial Library, Yale University. Her husband had died about two months previously, and she was nine months pregnant at the writing of these entries. The child who was subsequently born, Joshua, was the child mourned so intensely in a passage quoted earlier in this chapter.

* * *

"Yesterday was the anniversary of our dear little Normans birth & my thoughts have been much upon him and upon my own severe illness [childbearing] at the time; & now that I am daily expecting to pass through a similar scene of trial I am led to examine myself with regard to the results of it. I then thought myself nearer to Eternity than ever before & my constitution was then so much weakened by protracted illness & suffering that I cannot but think it doubtful whether it will sustain another trial. I know not what my feelings would be, were I assured that the day of suffering would also prove the day of death, but I have thought much of it & have endeavored to prepare my mind for such a result; but I find I can only trust myself into the arms of my Saviour, & believe that if he designs to take me hence to be here no more forever, that he will give me dying grace whenever it is requisite. At no time does death ever seem so near, as when I am expecting from day to day to be laid upon a bed of suffering. . . ."

Diary of Mary White, unpublished manuscript, Huntington Library, entry of February 21, 1841.

* * *

". . . Think much about my future. Now that my sickness is so near I must think. I do wonder if I am prepared to die. I lack the simple childlike faith in Christ that I long for. I am afraid I rest on my own feelings and experiences. . . ."

Diary of Mrs. Charles C. Carpenter, unpublished filmed copy, Public Archives of Canada, Ottawa, entry of September 23, 1863. Her baby was born October 25.

* * * * * * *

Most of the diary entries in the sample that mention fear of dying were written during pregnancy. People did not, in the earlier part of the century, call the delivery process "delivering" or "childbirth." At least until 1865 diarists in the sample typically called it "sickness" (e.g., Mrs. Carpenter) or "illness" (e.g., Linka Keyser, Mary White) or being on a "bed of suffering" (e.g., Mary White).

Some male diarists felt trepidation when a wife, daughter, sister, or sister-in-law was near the time of childbirth. A substantial proportion of the male diarists lost a wife, daughter, sister, or sister-in-law in childbirth or as a result of complications afterward. So childbirth was seen by both women and men as a time of vulnerability, and the most blessed aspect of a blessed event might have been that the woman survived. But trepidation does not seem to have affected grief.

As far as can be determined from the diary material, four of the 33 male diarists in the sample lost wives in childbirth, or as a result of complications from childbirth or spontaneous abortion. For only two of those four are there diary entries in the three years after the death. These two cases do not provide a sufficient base for generalizing, but in their diary entries neither man expressed any sense of expecting or anticipating the death (in both cases the women had borne children previously). A comparison of the emotional tone of the husbands' first reports of loss with the tone of their diary entries at other times (and with the tone of their other initial reports of loss) shows that both men were extremely distraught at the deaths in childbirth.

* * * * * * *

"On this sad day the Episode of my life which on the 14th of Aug, 1841, opened so auspiciously, & continued for two years so happily, was brought to a painful close — my dearest Harriet, my earthly all in all, was taken away from this earth."

Diary of Henry Scadding, unpublished manuscript, Metropolitan Toronto Central Library, entry of September 26, 1843.

* * *

"I am compelled to chronicle here the sadest [sic] event of my life. Nothing could have happened to me that would have been more so. My wife was taken sick about mid night. About 6 o'clk her child was born. About 9 she died. The poor child is alive & well. O what a day . . . what is this world to me now? Were it not for my four poor helpless motherless children. They must be taken care of." Entry of March 7, 1868.

"Lonely Lonely day & dreary enough home." Entry of March 8, 1868.

"Don't feel as tho I cared whether the work was done or not — Were it not for my children I would not try to keep house. . . ." Entry of March 13, 1868.

Diary of Edward Bolivar Drew, unpublished manuscript. Minnesota Historical Society.

* * * * * * *

There is no evidence in the diaries of Scadding and Drew of muted grief reactions. Nor is there evidence of muted grief in diaries that dealt with a death of a daughter (Matthews) or a daughter-in-law (Hempstead) in childbirth. Admittedly the basis of evaluation is subjective. From the way the diarists reacted to other losses, one may attempt to establish a subjective basis of comparison. Given that crude measurement, if there were some expectation of death there was no obvious psychological withdrawal from the pregnant woman that caused the diarists' grief over the death in childbirth to be muted.

The absence of diary material dealing directly or indirectly with expectations of maternal death may mean that people did not expect a woman who was delivering a child to die. After all, most pregnancies did not end in maternal death. But the failure to express expectations may also indicate an unwillingness to be pessimistic or disloyal. It is certainly clear from the fears of some of the pregnant diarists that they had a genuine sense of the risks of childbearing, and Richard F. Matthews said that his daughter, who died in child-birth, left a will "if she should die in childbirth" (entry of May 30, 1881, unpublished manuscript, Metropolitan Toronto Central Library). That people who were bereaved by death of a woman in childbirth failed to express an expectation of the death may indicate that they had minimal awareness of the dangers of childbirth, that they were aware that most women survived, or that they were aware of the possibility of death and unwilling to write down something that would be disloyal or terrifying. Thus, the exploration of the place of high maternal death rate in the psychology of death-related feelings fails to reveal anything about the role of expectations in grief; the expectations of people who eventually became bereaved and the possible effects of unreported expectations cannot be documented. It is clear that some women feared the worst, and the documentation of this fear in the diaries provides a poignant sense of what it was like to be pregnant in those times. But no insight into grief processes can be obtained by exploring the consequences for the diarists in the sample of high maternal death rates.

Terminal Care and Grief

Terminal care is, in the diary data, too entangled with closeness of relationships and with coresidence for an unambiguous analysis of the effect of terminal care on grieving. When diarists wrote about providing terminal care it was usually for a closely related household member, whereas the instances of death in which the provision of care was not mentioned tended to involve more distant relatives who were not members of the household. Moreover, failure to mention involvement in nursing the seriously ill is, as was said in Chapter 4, open to several interpretations. Perhaps the diarist did not participate in nursing, or participated but did not think it appropriate to include in the diary. Only three of the deaths reported in the diaries occurred during hospitalization (two Civil War deaths and one in 1893, and prior to the 1893 hospital death of his wife, Corwin Snow was intensively involved in care for her outside the hospital). So the diary data provide no useful comparisons for examination of the effects of terminal care on grief processes in general. However, the documentation of involvement in terminal care is fascinating in itself and provides an interesting perspective on a phenomenon that historians have speculated about, the apparent preoccupation of North Americans with death from the latter part of the eighteenth century until well into the nineteenth.

Many of the diarists described their care for the dying, their presence at a deathwatch, their participation in the preparation of a corpse for burial (cf. Douglas, 1977, chap. 6; Habenstein & Lamers, 1962, chap. 6), or their involvement in a reburial. The diarists had much more contact with dying and the dead than do contemporary North Americans.

* * * * * * *

"It is a sad trail [sic] for my Father as no one realized she was really ill and Mary was sitting up with her while my Father went to bed, she seemed to die in her sleep. John and the boys arrived, poor boys saw their dear Grandmama and were much upset. George got here at daybreak; at three my dear Mother was laid in her last resting place, my dear brothers all assisted to put her in her coffin and carried it into the sitting room where we all kissed her for the last time. My brothers screwed the coffin down, Mary had cut out a cross and covered it with artificial flowers and put it on top of the coffn. My dear boys went with their uncles as mourners. My poor Father read the service, a fearful trial. John and the boys returned to 'Northbrook' after the funeral, I shall remain with my dear Father for some time."

Diary of Sarah Hallen Drinkwater, unpublished transcript, Archives of Ontario, Toronto, entry of February 2, 1864.

* * *

"Towards the last she begged us to pray for her release. 'Ma, are you praying?' 'Sister, are you praying?' Miss Libby read the 14th [chapter] of John, after which I tried to pray. Had she not asked me I could not have done it, but all along I had granted all her requests & should I fail now? After prayer they sang 'Jesus, Lover of My Soul.' Before they got through singing she asked to be turned over and died without further struggle. I rejoiced that her soul was delivered, that her sufferings were over, that she had gone home to God. . . ."

Diary of Dolly Lunt Burge (1962, p. 86) entry of October 6, 1863.

* * *

"Night found and kept us, dear Ma and I by the side of our dead."

Diary of Richard F. Matthews, postal clerk in London, Ontario, whose "dead" was a grown daughter who had died shortly after giving birth. Unpublished manuscript, Metropolitan Toronto Central Library, entry of May 28, 1881.

* * *

"done baking cake, bread, pies & cookies &c. this morning Jackson Sullivan came for me to go & set up with corpse (Mr. Johnson's girl.) sat up all night. cold snow all day."

Diary of Emily Hawley Gillespie, unpublished transcript, Iowa Historical Society, Iowa City, entry of November 23, 1861.

* * *

"I must put down the worst first to get it off my mind if possible. Before three this morning Mrs. Carden came for me to sit up with Barbary the rest of the night, which I did. She died this afternoon after a great deal of pain & misery. I *do* think she has suffered as much as a human being could suffer. As soon as she died, by John's request, brother [a physician] made a post mortem examination. While he was doing it Mrs. Carden went there . . . to lay her out, & of course was perfectly taken aback. Em has ever since been in a great way about it, is going to sleep with me tonight. I cannot bear to think or write any more about it, so away with the subject & to something pleasanter! . . ."

Diary of P. Adeline Brisbane, unpublished manuscript, State Historical Society of Wisconsin, entry of December 1, 1857. At the time of this entry the diarist was 16 years old.

* * *

"I performed the sad duty this afternoon of removing the remains of my dear babe Mary Julia to the Spring Grove Cemetery. It is the first grave dug on those grounds, & to night she sleeps alone among those peaceful groves. The corpse was very much decayed; & it was a sad sight to see, to what that once beautiful child is now reduced. Alas! What is life? What is beauty? The spirit, that is life; that is the beautiful, and I hope yet to see my beautiful babe with a form incorruptible & that fadeth not away."

Diary of William H. Brisbane, unpublished manuscript, State Historical Society of Wisconsin, entry of September 1, 1845.

* * * * * * *

The great contact the diarists had with dying and the dead makes the apparent "preoccupation" of people of the nineteenth century with death more understandable. Historians have made it clear that for the latter part of the eighteenth century and the early part of the nineteenth, North Americans were preoccupied with death in the sense that death occupied what seems to be an unusually large proportion of space in letters, diaries, sermons, and published writings (Aries, 1974; Douglas, 1977, chap. 6; Saum, 1974; Vinovskis, 1976). Although there were religious reasons for this apparent preoccupation, it may also have reflected people's greater contact with the dying and with corpses. The kind of contact Phoebe Brisbane described in one of the passages quoted above would be extraordinarily rare for a twentieth-century North American sixteen-year-old. Simply in terms of time spent in contact with dying and death, the diarists in the sample would have far more of these subjects to report in their letters than would North Americans in the twentieth century. It is, therefore, understandable that nineteenth-century North Americans would devote more writing to dying and death than people today. It would also make a letter containing a detailed factual report of a death seem less bizarre, since one could assume that the recipient of the letter would not be unfamiliar with such detail.

Death certainly had a fascination for many of the diarists, though that fascination may be different from what one can observe among contemporary North Americans. The fascination of death for the diarists seems to have arisen out of curiosity about the fate of the soul of the dying. Would the dying person show religious attitudes predictive of a better chance of going to heaven? Seeing a person die might also have helped one think about preparing for one's own death, though the preparation might not have been in the sense of being a good patient and well-behaved dying loved one, but rather in being a penitent.

Death in the nineteenth century, as implied in the discussion in chapter 4 on anticipatory grief, might also have been relatively unpredictable. People might more often have been unsure whether an illness was terminal; that too might have led to stronger curiosity about dying. Saum (1974) has also suggested that, because of the poor medical knowledge of that time and the absence of competent medical practitioners, lay people were interested in medical knowledge. Observing a dying and death, and even post-mortem signs, might have helped to deal with future medical crises.

One might expect guilt (regret or self-reproach over a possible breach of conduct in relation to the lost person) to arise from involvement in the medical care of people who subsequently died. There is almost no evidence in the diaries that someone who provided medical care for a person who subsequently died thought that failure to use the right treatment or to call a doctor soon enough might have contributed to the death. People who gave medical care at home seemed generally to feel that they had done or had tried to do a great deal for the deceased. Perhaps that relieved survivors of feelings of guilt. Parkes (1975a, p. 129), in his study of twentieth-century widows, found that women who had long preparation for a spouse's death seemed to feel less guilt, and this seemed to arise in part from devoted and self-sacrificing attention to the spouse during his dying.

Guilt seemed to be present or possibly present for only eight of the 142 deaths (6%). By contrast, Glick, Weiss, and Parkes reported, in a study of contemporary younger widows in the Boston area, that 14% expressed some self-reproach in connection with a spouse's death (1974, p. 57). Perhaps guilt, though experienced, seldom got into diaries; the diarist declined to write about it. Some diarists may have been inclined to admit feeling guilty only if they failed to bear their agony with religious fortitude (cf. Scott, 1970, p. 10). Admitting that they felt guilt about the death would have led them to feel guilty about their guilt because it might seem that they were questioning God's will. Or perhaps guilt was present in the diaries but in such a disguised form that it cannot be recognized. Occasions for guilt over a death may, however, have been less common in nineteenth-century North America. The instances of such guilt in the sample of diarists tend to be like the following from the diaries of Mary Richardson Walker and Thomas Edmonds, who were both living at a substantial distance from a relative at the time she died.

* * * * * * *

"A letter from sister Charlotte brings the news of my Mother's death which occured [sic] the 26 of February 1843. I had as I thought already buried my friends so that I imagined I should hardly reallize [sic] their death when it should occur, but I find this is not the case. I feel very sensibly the loss of my mother. I would adopt the words of Cowper, "My Mother—when I heard that thou was dead" &c. May I believe her spirit does indeed hover over her sorrowing child. . . . Everything calls her to mind. The image of her is vividly impressed on my imagination. I think of so much I would have written her & altho I never expected to see her myself again, I had fondly hoped my children would. But she is gone. Such dreams all vanish. I am thankful we had such a mother to lose. . . ."

Diary of Mary Richardson Walker, entry of July 18, 1844 (1963, p. 270).

* * *

"After a friend has left us, and gone to the world of the Spirits, without having communed with her in her Last Sickness, our breasts are filled with many additional regrets. . . ."

Diary of Thomas Edmonds, February 16, 1844. Unpublished manuscript, Huntington Library, San Marino, CA. Edmonds in this passage is writing of the death of his sister-in-law. His illness prevented him from attending her funeral.

* * * * * * *

Guilt may be hidden in the diaries or simply have been unreported. But it appears that the diarists most often felt guilt over failure to be present at a death or to attend a funeral. There apparently was a strong obligation to show caring and pay respect to the dying and the dead by being present at the death and the funeral. Failure to meet this obligation seemed the principal source of guilt feelings.

Summary

This chapter started out with theoretical questions about the linkage of medicine in the nineteenth century with grief. If medicine was so inadequate that many young children and many childbearing women died, would people steel themselves for such deaths in a way that muted grief? If most medical care in the nineteenth century involved family care for terminally ill members, would that affect grief, particularly by increasing guilt over a death?

The expectation of a relatively high likelihood of death for a young child seemed to have no effect on grief. During the early part of the nineteenth century, when the deaths of infants and young children were particularly common, there was no less grief for infants and young children than during the latter part of the century. An examination of the premises and documentation offered by some scholars who have argued that the deaths of young children might have little impact on people when the death rate for this age group is high suggests that those arguments may not have been well founded. Children were important to people in the nineteenth century, in some ways particularly so to women, and child deaths were not predictable.

The expectation of a relatively high likelihood of death for women in childbirth also seemed to have no effect on grief, but there are insufficient cases in the diary sample to provide firm support for the assertion of no effect. It is clear from the diary data that many people were quite aware of the risks of childbirth. Most of the diary data on fear of death came from pregnant women, and the risks were also reflected in how people wrote about childbirth.

Many of the diarists participated in the medical care of dying kin and neighbors; apparently only three of 142 deaths in the diary material occurred in a hospital. There were reports of deaths in which the diarists did not provide nursing care for the deceased, but those deaths were of people generally not living with the diarist and also more distantly related. Without variability on the dimension of hospital versus home death, it is impossible to make comparisons holding relationship with the deceased constant. Nonetheless, the heavy involvement of diarists with dying and the dead makes the preoccupation with death of eighteenth- and nineteenth-century North Americans more understandable.

When the diary data are probed for guilt over errors in medical care, no guilt of that sort can be found. However, there are indications that the failure to provide care, to be present at the time a close relative was dying, or to attend a funeral was a source of guilt feelings.

6

The Time Course of Grief for Deaths and Separations

Changes over Time in Grief for Deaths and Separations

"Got letter . . . *Mamas Death Oh!* how bad, shocking, got excused from duty and passed it (the letter) [to] Addy. . . . Letter was from Nellie. Wrote home this eve. . . . Feeling sad but not so much as I would have expected. *God helping me.* . . . God help my sister and Father, and me. We all need it." (entry of September 25, 1863)

"Bright & pleasant—feeling sad and lonely. My heart is full. I have begun to realize 'I am *motherless*' Oh! What an affliction. I can hardly sit still thinking of her all day. My heart aches most all day. Heard by George's letter [that] she died with Dyssentary. . . . Not feeling so sad this eve." (September 26, 1863)

". . . . Feeling better in spirits but sad enough. . . ." (September 27, 1863)

". . . . Not feeling so sad to day, don't realize while at work, busy all day. . . ." (September 28, 1863)

Diary of Alfred F. Armstrong, Civil War soldier from Michigan, unpublished manuscript at Archives of Ontario, Toronto.

* * *

Second day of grief

"I had a troubled sleep and woke before 5. Just as soon as I thought of my grief I could not sleep again. I tho't of dear little Abbie weeping for her darling. I tho't of the poor boy in his delirium calling for his dear ones. I wonder if my name was even on his lips. O my brother. I did not think when I saw you in Worcester on that last day that I should see your face no more on earth. Poor happy George. O if I only knew he was safe in heaven. . . . It was a sad day.

72

I could not forget for a minute, and the tears would come. I pray that this may be sanctified tears and that we may not fail to get the lesson God would teach. . . ."

Third day of grief

"Sunday . . . I could not help crying. Everything reminded me of him. I tho't too of Adeline River. She is dead. I did not think she could die. . . . Oh! . . . . I took my Bible, & one of the first things I saw was a passage Geo had himself marked. . . ."

Fourth day of grief

"My heart is full of tho'ts of George."

Fifth day of grief

". . . In my room alone I met Jesus. I cast my care on Him, my dark feelings I leave with Him. I do thank Him that He has mingled so much comfort in my cup of sorrow. I have been reading our dear George's letters. They do speak comfort to my heart. . . ."

Sixth day of grief

". . . I have given all I have to give in the States to my Country. My dear Geo is beyond the strife of war. . . . In looking over the Boston Journal I see my dear George's name amg. the dead. . . . It made the tears fall."

Ninth day of grief

". . . . This poor heart aches still. I must think it all over and over. The weary nights and days of the 7 long weeks in which he suffered alone. God knows what is best. I hope I do not rebel. O I cannot write out what I thought as I read [?] all—dear mother's letter. . . ."

Sixteenth day of grief

"As I was working over those apples [just received from home], I tho't continually of home and Geo. I could not keep the tears back. I am afraid I do wrong in feeling so deeply. I ought to be so thankful that I have such hope in his death. I hope I do not grieve the dear Savior by my grief. O that it might lead me near to Him! I cannot, it seems to me doubt but Geo was a [Christian]. His life should be the test not his death. O for grace! . . . Am thinking, thinking, thinking tonight of the 2 graves in our dear cemetery instead of one. Who will go next?"

Seventeenth day of grief

". . . . Tho't much all day about Geo. I realize more & more each day what is gone. I talked a long time with [my husband Charles] about him. My heart aches, but I thank God."

Diary of Mrs. Charles C. Carpenter, unpublished photocopied manuscript at Public Archives of Canada, Ottawa, excerpts of entries from June 13 to 28, 1863.

* * *

"Heaven does not look so near to me as it did. I have come back in some measure. The wound bleeds & will while life lasts, but the first anguish is exchanged for a suffering as real, but less intense. I see him in all. I miss him in all. The restless agony of my sleeping moments has yielded to a watchfulness less disturbed, and the tears & groans of a heart alive to sorrow while the senses are slumbering, have in a good degree ceased. But I mourn. My precious husband is dearer than I ever knew him to be in life. . . . (October 12, 1819)

"It is a great grief & trouble to me that after having experienced *such* a trial, so calculated to detach me from *this* world, I find I have an earthy heart still. I want *now* to live one day at a time. . . . I find myself saying, 'When shall I fix my place of *future* residence. How shall I ever do my duty to all these children. How shall I manage to make my little property turn to the most advantageous account'. . . ." (October 31, 1819)

Diary of Susan Mansfield Huntington, unpublished manuscript, Manuscripts and Archives Division, Sterling Memorial Library, Yale University. Huntington's husband had died about September 7, 1819.

* * * * * * *

Even in the relatively short span covered by the excerpts from the Armstrong, Carpenter, and Huntington diaries, it seems clear that the grief of each of the diarists was changing over time. A more precise analysis of all the diary data indicates that the average level of grief dropped considerably in the first few months following a loss. Table 6.1 lists the proportions of entries for each of the first 36 months following a loss that contain some indication of grief for the lost person. It is evident in that table that by the third year following a loss, grief for a specific lost person is very rare. This suggests that for many losses the diarists had completed or nearly completed their grief work, that other aspects of their lives had become more salient. It should be recalled, however, that data and arguments presented in Chapter 2 indicate that grief for some losses can hit peaks of great intensity years after a death.

The death of anyone, particularly a person close to one, is so horrible, so appalling, so permanent that it may seem irreverent and insensitive to ask whether grief over a separation might be greater than grief over a death. Yet a separation, even though it may lack the initial horror of a death (and it may not always), may in the long run weigh more constantly on one's mind than a death. When someone has died nothing can be done to restore the person to life. The possibility of communication, even if one is a spiritist (several diarists in the sample were; see Chapter 10) is limited. Living as

Table 6.1. Proportion of Entries with Grief for the Lost Person

Month	Deaths		Separations	
	Proportion with Grief for Lost Person	Number of Deaths	Proportion with Grief for Lost Person	Number of Separations
1	.147	127	.056	170
2	.060	115	.025	156
3	.040	105	.021	121
4	.016	98	.022	103
5	.010	101	.017	90
6	.017	100	.017	85
7	.018	100	.020	78
8	.007	92	.011	69
9	.023	96	.019	54
10	.002	97	.014	54
11	.025	95	.005	56
12	.013	92	.009	52
13	.021	92	.013	51
14	.001	85	.013	46
15	.007	89	.005	48
16	.004	82	.006	41
17	.000	84	.011	35
18	.004	84	.016	35
19	.002	89	.024	34
20	.003	88	.011	35
21	.001	84	.010	31
22	.012	81	.010	28
23	.014	82	.008	21
24	.012	83	.007	20
25	.002	82	.004	27
26	.007	79	.010	27
27	.014	76	.029	22
28	.000	80	.027	26
29	.001	82	.006	23
30	.002	81	.007	22
31	.004	75	.011	19
32	.006	77	.023	19
33	.002	71	.013	18
34	.006	71	.003	19
35	.001	68	.004	15
36	.000	63	.010	16

though the dead would return is impractical and potentially very risky; one is under pressure to live in a world in which the dead person is really dead. But in the case of separation, communication may continue; reunion, even if it would require many months of travel, is possible; and the door cannot be closed or can be closed only with difficulty on the separated. Thus, in the long run, grief over a separation may be more intense than grief over a death.

The month-by-month grief data in Table 6.1 clearly show that in the first three months following loss grief is substantially greater for deaths than for separations. Then, for the next 21 months, grief is greater for death in about half the months and greater for separations in about half the months. In the third year, however, though the differences are small, grief is greater for separations than for deaths in 11 of the 12 months.

Changes over Time in Mentions of the Lost

Although the irreversibility of death might lead to relatively intense and long-term grieving, the continued existence of a lost person might lead to more frequent linking of dates and current events to the lost person than in the case of a death. The continued existence of a person, even one who is geographically distant, usually enables (and perhaps even requires) some sort of communication with that person. This communication might well receive substantial comment in the typical diary. Moreover, the continued existence of a separated family member may require one to make decisions with that person in mind and to plan for possible future interactions. Thus, if the continued existence of a separated person leads by the third year of loss to greater grieving, it might also lead much earlier in bereavement to greater thinking of the lost. Thus, deaths and separations would probably be even more strongly differentiated on the dimension of mentioning of a lost person than on the dimension of grief for the lost person.

Table 6.2 contains a summary of the data on mentions of the lost. It can be seen in this table that in every month after the first following a loss there are proportionately more mentions of a separated person than of a dead person. Thus, the data on mentions of the lost support the notion that, in the long run, a dead person becomes more nearly removed from one's thinking than one who is alive

Table 6.2. Proportion of Entries Mentioning the Lost Person

	Deaths		Separations	
Month	Proportion Mentioning Lost Person	Number of Deaths	Proportion Mentioning Lost Person	Number of Separations
1	.329	127	.206	170
2	.100	115	.118	156
3	.074	105	.095	121
4	.052	98	.090	103
5	.053	101	.112	90
6	.042	100	.100	85
7	.048	100	.099	78
8	.027	92	.071	69
9	.042	96	.076	54
10	.042	97	.089	54
11	.046	95	.088	56
12	.034	92	.061	52
13	.068	92	.081	51
14	.009	85	.076	46
15	.026	89	.075	48
16	.017	82	.084	41
17	.010	84	.103	35
18	.018	84	.073	35
19	.011	89	.102	34
20	.011	88	.123	35
21	.022	84	.082	31
22	.020	81	.083	28
23	.025	82	.063	21
24	.025	83	.040	20
25	.021	82	.156	27
26	.014	79	.053	27
27	.030	76	.171	22
28	.011	80	.162	26
29	.021	82	.100	23
30	.013	81	.060	22
31	.013	75	.051	19
32	.012	77	.077	19
33	.022	71	.109	18
34	.026	71	.190	19
35	.019	68	.184	15
36	.007	63	.175	16

but physically distant. In that sense a separation may weigh more heavily on one than a death.

Approximately 50% of the mentions of people lost through separation seem to be related to communication—communications sent, received, not sent or not received, communication plans, or a review of communications recently sent or received. In contrast, only about 9% of the mentions of people lost through death seem to be related to communication (including letters received or sent that mention the deceased). The importance of communication in separation reinforces the notion that one can do the grief work for a loss due to death more completely than for a loss through separation.

The difference in significance of communication for the two kinds of losses also raises a question: What would happen if transportation failure or ignorance of the current residence of someone from whom one was separated made communication impossible? If the break in communication were apparently permanent, the grief process might well follow the time course of the grief process for death. But, as the data analyzed in this chapter seem to indicate, that process might lead to somewhat earlier completion of grief work or to a more nearly complete end of emotional distress over the loss. If so, and if people were aware of that and found grief punishing, perhaps they would be tempted not to communicate with people lost through separation. Although no diarist hinted at that, there might be some temptation to end communication in order to finish with the relationship and with grieving. However, the following quote from the diary of a Wisconsin farmer may represent the way most diarists felt about communication during separation.

* * * * * * *

"How great is the privilege of being able to converse with distant friends through the medium of paper, pen & ink; were it not for this, separation from friends would amount to banishment."

Diary of Dustin G. Cheever, unpublished manuscript, Whitewater Regional Historical Center, State Historical Society of Wisconsin, entry of July 5, 1851. During the nineteenth century the word "friends" often encompassed relatives.

* * * * * * *

It can be seen in Table 6.2 that for all but one month after the 13th, the proportion of diary entries mentioning individuals from whom the diarists were separated is more than twice the proportion of entries mentioning deceased individuals. That helps in understanding the meaning of the high proportion of entries mentioning separated individuals in which some aspect of the flow of communication between the individuals appears to have been a cause of the mention. Subtracting the entries in which communication with the separated was mentioned from all entries mentioning the lost still leaves a higher rate of mentions for separations than for deaths. Communication may have been one mechanism that made grief work slower, less appropriate, and less desired in the case of separation. But it is clear that when the direct effect of communication flow is removed from the data, people lost through separation still tended in the long run to play a more prominent part in the diary records than dead people.

Implications of Comparisons of Deaths and Separations

The fact that the monthly proportions of entries for grief and for mentions show similar patterns for separations and deaths should come as no surprise to people familiar with the work of Bowlby (e.g., 1961, 1980) and of Marris (1974). Both have argued that a variety of losses besides death can produce grieflike processes. This is true, Marris argued (1974), even for desired changes, and in the lives of the diarists many of the separations seem to have been desired. A move might have brought somebody to a desired vocation or to a larger or more productive plot of land. But for the diarists, even desired separations brought grief for people from whom they were separated. For example, Mary Richardson Walker had wanted fervently to become a missionary. In an era in which single women of her denomination were not permitted to do mission work, she had agreed to marry a man, after extremely brief contact, because he was interested in such work. As the day approached when she was to marry and leave New England for the Oregon Territory she wrote, "My mind is full of tender thoughts on bid[ding] adieu to home. It is indeed trying" (1963, p. 40, entry of December 17, 1837).

The finding of somewhat greater grief in the long run for separations than for deaths implies that grief should not be underestimated for people with any kind of long-term separation—including, for example, relatives of missing-in-action soldiers, of people with long-term prison sentences, of missing persons, of ethnographic field-workers, and of emigrants. Occasional face-to-face contact, as is sometime the case with, say, families of convicts, may complicate the matter. Does each new separation start a new grieving process? Does the occasional contact simply punctuate a single long process? (In the present study a face-to-face contact was counted as ending a separation, even if it was only a moment of contact amid years of noncontact.) For families in which there is a burden of long-term separation, the data on grieving suggest that in the long run grieving is more frequent than if the person had died, and the data on mentions indicate that the separated will be more in people's awareness than if the person had died.

The consequences for social life and day-to-day activities of the slow accommodation to a separation are undoubtedly complex. It may be that for a separation, as opposed to a death, others may be less likely to be recruited to fill the role of the missing person or less likely to be committed to such a role if they assume it. People may be reluctant to develop a life pattern in which an absent person who had been close to them would, if returned, have no part. Although accepting a role previously held by someone who died, accepting someone else in the role, or coming to grips with the idea that nobody will ever occupy the role may be part of grieving in the case of a death, dealing with one's reluctance, inability, or difficulty in recruiting a role substitute or with the lower commitment of a temporary substitute may be part of the grief load in the case of a separation.

7

Separations:
Leavers vs. Left

In separations, often at least one person is a leaver and at least one person is left. (On occasion, everybody leaves, but some go in different directions from others.) The distinction between leaver and left has been usefully explored both for the ending of courtship relations and for divorce (Goode, 1965; Hill, Rubin & Peplau, 1976; Nevaldine, 1978; Waller, 1967; Weiss, 1975). Leavers may feel more guilt; people who are left may feel more pain and anger and may in some ways be more passive. But both leavers and left often feel something that could be called grief.

Among the diarists, a leaver is defined as a person who moved to a place a substantial distance from another for at least four weeks. A person who was left is defined as one who remained in a dwelling and was left by someone for at least four weeks. Although both leaver and left may have felt grief, a case can be made for the person who was left feeling more grief at first. The left would have continued to be surrounded by stimuli that were reminders of the leaver. Such stimuli seem to be, as the discussion of anticipatory grief in Chapter 4 and as several studies suggest (Parkes, 1972, p. 67; Rosenblatt, Walsh, & Jackson, 1976, chaps. 3, 4), powerful in producing feelings of grief. The leaver, by contrast, would not have had many stimuli setting off thoughts of the lost. So it could be argued that in the early days, weeks, and months of grieving, a person who was left would mention the lost person, and show grief, in proportionately more diary entries than a leaver. The leaver may also have been preoccupied with the business of traveling, living in new settings, and perhaps engaging in new types of work (see, for example, Faragher's 1979 analysis of the preoccupying trials of the Overland Trail). This preoccupation may have directed a leaver's thoughts away from specific relationship losses, so that grief over any specific loss might have been less. A leaver's preoccupation with novelty may also have dominated diary entries; novel sights and experiences may have taken up most or all of the diary-writing energy and the available page space, leaving little space for grief over loss. A contradictory argument might also be made, on the grounds that the leaver lost much more than the left (other relationships, the dwelling, possessions, perhaps the home country) and was more likely to be without any previous coresidents. But it is difficult to see how grief over all other losses would lead to increased frequency of mention of a specific loss, unless it served as a symbol for all the others. It seems more reasonable to expect people who have been left to grieve more than leavers.

Table 7.1. First Month of Separation for Leavers and Left

	Proportion of Entries Mentioning Lost		Proportion of Entries with Grief for Lost	
	Left	Leaver	Left	Leaver
All cases	.279	.145	.066	.048
Diarist 30 or younger	.412	.204	.091	.092
Diarist older than 30	.252	.095	.061	.011
Diarist older than 30 and living with lost	.276	.117	.070	.012
Diarist older than 30 and not living with lost	.083	.063	.000	.010

When the data are examined, the speculative analysis of grief in separations receives some support. It can be seen in the top row of the right-hand side of Table 7.1 that in the first month of loss, diarists who were left showed a somewhat higher proportion of entries with grief than diarists who were leavers (.066 vs .048 entries), but the difference is unimpressive. However, when the data on mentions of the lost are examined, there is a much larger difference. The person who was left was much more likely than the leaver to mention the lost person (in .279 of the entries vs .145 of the entries).

As further corroboration of the theoretical analysis, leavers wrote more entries during the first month of separation than did people who were left (24.15 vs 21.00). From this it could be inferred that the leavers had more going on in their lives, and more days on which noteworthy things happened. Yet the leavers less often mentioned specific people from whom they were separated than the people who were left (2.43 vs 4.73). The leavers were apparently preoccupied with the novelty of their move or with other losses.

The fact that the data on grief appear to show a smaller difference between leaver and left than do the data on mentions suggests that reminders have a stronger influence on one's thoughts of a lost person than on grief for that person. Reminders may work in the grief process through an intermediary stage of thinking about the lost person. There may at times be a direct linkage, or what is experienced as a direct linkage, between a reminder and grieving. But apparently reminders often lead to thinking of a lost person in a way that does not set off grief strong enough to show up in a diary entry. Reminders, in theory, may or may not set off thinking about a lost person, and when thinking does occur, it may or may not lead to grieving. Whether or not the thinking leads to grieving presumably depends on how much grief work has already been done in the areas one is thinking about. If the area does not involve memories and hopes connected to the lost, or if one has already done the grief work neutralizing the memories and hopes, one can think about the lost without substantial grieving.

The picture drawn so far of the differences and similarities between leaver and left may be a plausible one, but it is still too simple. Although the difference in grief between all people who were leavers and all who were left is a small one, further analysis of the diary data indicates that for some categories of persons, those who were left experienced substantially more grief than leavers. It can be seen, in the lower part of Table 7.1, that the diarist's age and residence with the lost person make a difference. Whereas leavers and people who were left did not differ in grief when age 30 or younger at the onset of loss, who were older than 30 did differ. It is not that being left made no difference to younger diarists. In fact the proportion of first-month diary entries with grief is higher for younger than for older diarists who were left. Rather, it is that leaving also yielded a comparatively high level of grief in younger diarists. Separation at an early age, whether the diarist was the leaver or the left, seems to have been distressing. Older diarists seem to have been less grief-stricken by a separation and to have reacted more strongly when they were left (when reminders were present) than when they were leavers.

In the bottom two lines of the right-hand side of Table 7.1 it can be seen that among the diarists over 30 at the onset of loss, those for whom there was a grief difference between leavers and left, the difference is actually present only among those who were living with the lost person at the time of separation. This finding is consistent with the theoretical analysis. Reminders of the lost person should be much more frequently present and salient if one had lived with the lost person and was still in the residence that had been shared. For people who were not living with the lost person before the separation, the proportions of entries with grief for leaver and for left are virtually identical. The lack of difference makes sense in that the presence of reminders in the immediate environment would be virtually identical for leavers and for left who were not living together.

To illustrate differences between leaver and left, there is only one instance in which two diarists who were both in the sample separated from each other. The example is imperfect for many reasons; the husband and wife differed in age (she was 27 at the time, he 33); they had not been long at the place where they were living when he left, and she was presumably under more stress than he, since she was pregnant and sharing the dwelling with many nonrelatives. The example is unique in many other ways, so there may be many factors other than leaver versus left that account for the differences in the two diarists' references to each other.

At the time of the entries quoted, September and October of 1838, the diarists had recently married and traveled overland from New England to the Oregon Territory to be missionaries. They separated temporarily when Elkanah, the husband, left Mary, the wife, in order to search out (in the company of another male missionary) a site at which to establish a mission. The pages quoted in the following are from diaries edited by Clifford M. Drury (M. Walker, 1963; E. Walker, 1976).

Mary	Elkanah
Sept. 10, 1838. ". . . . worked as hard as I could untill (sic) Mr. Walker got ready to start. . . . After crying a little, picked up & found myself somewhat tired." (p. 126)	Sept. 10, 1838. ". . . . it was hard to part with my wife, leaving her alone when her [condition] demanded more than ever my presence & attention." (p. 68)
Sept. 11 ". . . . good news from our husbands. Hope they will make a successful expedition." (p. 126)	
Sept. 16. ". . . . finished writing my letters home to Mr. W.'s folks. . . ." (p. 127)	
Sept. 17. ". . . . In the P.M. began to work on husband's coat. The Dr. hurried & bustled about just as my husband does. . . ." (p. 127)	
	Sept. 18. ". . . . I take much delight in writing this journal because my dear companion will read it with pleasure. It is for her sake that I write more than for my own gratification. I wish I could this night see her if nothing more, could hear from her. I long for the time to come when [we] shall meet again. I fear that some accident will befall her, but she is in the hands of our all wise and gracious God. . . ." (P. 75)
Sept. 19. "Mrs. Eells helped sew & we finished my Husb. coat. . . . My health is good and I enjoy myself quite well, only I want to see my good husband so. . . ." (p. 127)	Sept. 19. ". . . . begun letter to my dear companion or in other words to my wife." (p. 76)
Sept. 23. "Morning worship & family prayer meeting. . . . Every little while I would find my mind on my husband, it seems a long time already since he left, & longer still before he will return. I can hardly refrain from tears every time I think of him. I know I am foolish but I can't help it. I ought to be more [thankful] than I feel that I have so good a husband & that I have enjoyed his society so much; & not be sad because he is gone a little." (p. 128)	

Sept. 29. ". . . . We were hoping to hear from our husbands by this time. Mrs. E. manifests much solicitude about hers & I would at least like to hear from mine." (p. 129)

October 1. "Had letters from Messrs. W. & Eells. . . . Fear my husband will suffer for want of his coat." (p. 129)

Oct. 2. ". . . . I wish I knew whether my husband likes to have me pray before folks or not. When he comes home I will ask him. Fear when he comes home he will be disappointed to find me no more proficient in the language [Nez Perce]." (p. 129)

Oct. 4. ". . . . Mrs. Smith is worried for fear her husband will not get along so well [if] Mr. Walker & Eells are here. . . . I have finished all my letters & wish husband could read them before I send them away." (p. 129)

Oct. 6. ". . . . I was truly glad to find a letter from my wife, being the first I had heard from her since I left." (p. 92)

Oct. 7. ". . . . Have been searching my heart to-day to see how much sinfulness could be found there. Detect so much in others that I fear I do not see it quick in my self & husband, as I do elsewhere." (p. 130)

Oct. 8. ". . . . Wrote to husband. . . ." (p. 130)

Oct. 9. "Hear our husbands are at Mr. Spalding's. . . ." (p. 130)

Elkanah Walker returned on October 13. Only Mary's diary recorded the event: "Husband & Mr. Eells came about noon. Was glad once more to see my husband & he appears glad to see me & I suppose he really was for he has no faculty of making believe. Could not sleep all night for joy" (p. 131).

Elkanah actually wrote many more words in his diary during the separation than Mary wrote in hers, yet her entries dealt far more often with the separation than his. She seemed to mention him in a much higher proportion of entries for the separation than he mentioned her. She mentioned him in .40 of her entries during the separation, while he mentioned her in .10 of his entries during that time. But they grieved in the same proportion of entries—grief in .10 of their entries for the period of separation. The data they provided on mentions of the lost parallel the differences reported in Table 7.1; the person who was left (Mary) mentioned the lost person proportionately more often than did the leaver (Elkanah). The grief data are harder to evaluate, since Mary was under 30 and Elkanah was not. The grief data for this one example, if scored in terms of proportion of entries with grief, do not support the theoretical analysis. However, if the measure of grief were number of emotion-laden words referring to the lost or ratio of emotion-laden words to all words, then Mary would clearly be scored as having had more grief than Elkanah.

For all cases, people who were left tend to be significantly older than leavers (age 50 on the average versus age 38). Although leaving might involve a visit to distant relatives, a prolonged business trip, a tour of duty in the military, or some other probably temporary change, quite often it involved migration. As the data indicate, older people were less often leavers than were younger people (Faragher, 1979, chap. 2, also reported that older people were underrepresented among overland emigrants to the west coast of the United States). Older people tended to live in a more stable world geographically, and one can presume that people were usually aware that geographic mobility was greater for the young than for the old. From the point of view of the theoretical analysis comparing leavers with the left, one might suppose that the separation would be much harder on an older person who was left than on a younger person who was a leaver. However, as the data in Table 7.1 suggest, younger leavers actually seemed to experience more grief than older persons who were left.

8

Grief When There Is
More Grief Work to Be Done

According to the theory of grief work, losses are greater when there are more memories, hopes, and behavior patterns to be disconnected from the lost person. The "more grief work to be done" in the chapter title refers to situations in which there are many such memories, hopes, and behavior patterns to be disconnected. Of course people may not and need not feel greater grief the more there is to disconnect, and they may not and need not feel little grief when comparatively few disconnections are necessary.

This chapter deals only with deaths, not with separations. The disconnecting required by any given separation is difficult to assess. For some memories, hopes, and behavior patterns, separation itself may lead one to disconnect simply in order to function in one's daily environment. But for other hopes, memories, and behavior patterns, one may work at maintaining the connections because there is no need to disconnect; reunion is likely. In some cases, one may even work at maintaining the connections as a way of increasing the likelihood of renewing the relationship. Separations are thus too difficult to analyze from the viewpoint of the theory of grief work unless one can understand the nature and perceived future of the separation. That kind of understanding is not often possible with the diary data, so the analyses here focus on death.

The theory of grief work implies that the most difficult losses are of people one has known for a long time (more memories to disengage), of people long living with one (both more memories and more behavior patterns to disengage), and of people with whom one has had a complex rather than a simple relationship (more memories, behavior patterns, and perhaps hopes to disengage).

Closeness of Relationship

If closeness of relationship gives more memories, hopes, and behavior patterns to disconnect following a loss, it seems plausible to expect more grief over the months following the loss of someone close. However, the issue is by no means simple. Closeness probably brings with it more dependence, greater obligations to grieve, more economic loss following the death, and many other reasons for grieving that fall outside the scope of the theory of grief work. Nonetheless, it would be a striking failure of the theory if relationship closeness were not associated with grief.

Grief for deaths of people closely linked to a diarist (spouse, parent, offspring, or sibling) was compared with grief for all other deaths. Grief was greater for the closer relationship in every month in the first three years of bereavement in which there was at least some variability in grief. (If no diarists express grief in a given month of bereavement, one cannot say that grief is more likely to be present when the loss was of a close person or when anything else is true.) For 33 of the first 36 months, diarists showed grief for deaths of people with whom they had had close relationships, but for only two of the first 36 months of bereavement (the first and the thirteenth) was there grief for deaths of people who had not had a close relationship with a diarist. The data indicate overwhelmingly that closeness of relationship, as implied by the theory of grief work (and by considerations of economics, obligation, etc.), is associated with greater grief for a death. From another perspective, one of the costs of a close relationship is its potential for relatively great and long-term grief.

Coresidence

According to the theory of grief work, there would be more work to do if a coresident died. There would be more memories, behavior patterns, and perhaps hopes linked to a coresident. Thus, the theory of grief work would lead to the prediction of greater grief for deaths of coresidents.

For all deaths, coresidence is associated with greater grief in 19 of the first 24 months of bereavement (in four of the remaining five months, grief was greater without coresidence). In the third year of bereavement, grief was greater in five of the 12 months if bereaved and deceased lived together and less in five other of the 12 months if they did not. There was no grief in the diary entries for either kind of loss in the remaining two months. It would appear that coresidence led to greater grief in the first two years of bereavement. However, coresidence is related to closeness of relationship, which appears to be a source of greater grief. It therefore seems useful to look at the effects of coresidence, with relationship closeness held constant. However, for each specific type of close relationship—offspring, sibling, parent, and spouse—residence is generally the same. Diarists were almost invariably living with spouses and younger offspring who died. They were almost never living with older offspring, parents, and siblings who died. For more distant relationships (grandparent, cousin, etc.), there are too few instances of death, and coresidence was invariably rare. So there is no way to test the coresidence prediction holding relationship closeness constant. Even though coresidence seems associated with grief in the first two years of bereavement, the possibility that the apparent effect of coresidence is really due to kinship closeness cannot be ruled out.

Duration of Relationship

In longer relationships there should be more memories to disconnect. If hopes are ignored, the simple prediction of the theory of grief work is that the longer the relationship (and hence the more numerous the memories), the greater is one's grief when the relationship ends. In the following discussion, the duration-of-relationship implication of the theory of grief work is examined for each of the four closest kinship relationships in western culture—sibling, offspring, parent, and spouse.

Sibling Deaths

There are, in the diary data, 20 cases of sibling death. In 19 of the 20 cases, the diarist was not living with the sibling at the time of death, and in the other case residence cannot be determined. The age of the younger of two siblings would be an appropriate measure of the length of their relationship. However, there are so many cases with age of deceased sibling unknown that to use that measure would cut the sample of sibling deaths in half. Hence, it was decided to use diarist age as the measure of relationship duration in the case of sibling deaths. If the derivation from the theory of grief is valid, the data should show that the older the diarist the greater was grief for a deceased sibling. The data, however, show the opposite pattern. For all seven months in the first year of bereavement in which a diarist expressed grief for a sibling who had died (hence, the seven months in which there was some variability in grief to correlate with the variability in diarist age), the greater the diarist's age the less the grief. There was only one month beyond the first year in which grief was expressed by some diarist for a sibling who had died, which says something about the strength of connections with siblings living apart. For that one month, the 26th month of bereavement, the older the diarist the greater the grief. In sum, for seven of the eight months in which the data varied, the older the diarist the less the grief. However, the apparent contradiction of a derivation from the theory of grief work may be an artifact of difference in experience between older and younger diarists. Although the grief of a younger diarist may be more intense when everything else is held constant, in the present case the younger diarists had been separated from their siblings for a shorter time than the older diarists. Thus, the sibling data that seem to run counter to the derivation from the theory of grief work may only mean that the longer siblings have been living apart, the weaker their connections with each other.

Offspring Deaths

For parents grieving for a dead offspring, the measure of duration of relationship is obviously offspring age. There are, in the sample, 29 deaths of offspring, ranging in age from a few weeks to 53 years. If only memories are considered, the theory of grief work would lead to the prediction of greater parental grief the older the offspring. However, for the diarists the relationship of parental grief to offspring age depends on whether parent and offspring were living together at the time of offspring death. The pattern of data is indeterminate for coresident offspring (whose mean age was 4.6) but is quite clear for noncoresident offspring (whose mean age was 35.0). For noncoresident offspring the older the offspring the *less* the grief. This is true for 27 of 28 months across the three years immediately following the loss. (Statistical details are given in Appendix C.) Quite possibly for noncoresident offspring, the older the offspring the longer parent and offspring had been separated. If so, the older the offspring the fewer the memories and behavior patterns that were connected to the offspring and the fewer the hopes the parent had invested in the offspring's future at the time of death.

The offspring data suggest several amendments to the theory of grief work. First of all, the data on noncoresident offspring, like the data on siblings, suggest that it is not merely the amount of time for accumulating memories that governs grief. Rather, one must take into account how well connected people are when one of them dies. People who have not been sharing a residence have fewer linkages of behavior patterns, and apparently the residential separation leads to some disconnecting of memories (or reminders of memories). Thus the relationship of age of offspring at time of death to parent grief when the offspring was not living with the parent may reflect a history of disconnecting that began when residences were separated. Furthermore, the data on noncoresident offspring seem to imply that the hopes Freud wrote about are more heavily invested in younger persons. Those hopes include, no doubt, a complex set of fantasies and expectations concerning future parent-offspring interaction. That too may account for the finding of greater grief for younger noncoresident offspring.

The data on coresident offspring are inconsistent with the prediction from the theory of grief work, which may mean that memories and hopes are counterpoised. The more hope a parent has for a child the fewer the memories; the more memories the fewer the hopes. Hopes are highest, one can speculate, when children are comparatively young and the parent has a comparatively small number of memories of the child. Although one can interpret Freud's analysis of mourning as saying that hopes and memories are somehow additive, they may actually change in relative importance over the course of a relationship. The cumulative effect of memories, as a close relationship goes on, may eventually outweigh the reduction in hopes. If

this is so, and if the typical coresident offspring had died at a substantially greater age, there might have been greater grief in the
latter part of the first three years of bereavement the older the
offspring was at time of death.

Parent Deaths

Thirteen of the 16 deaths of parents for whom residence at time
of death can be determined occurred when parent and offspring were
not living together. Again, focusing primarily on memories, the
theory of grief work would seem to predict that the older the offspring (and hence the longer the relationship) the greater would be
the offspring's grief at the parent's death. After the second month of
grief, there is very little grief expressed by any offspring for a dead
parent, so there is not much opportunity for a statistical trend to
appear. There are data variations for four months in the first year of
loss and for two in the second. For five of those six months the older
the diarist the less the grief for the dead parent. The data are meager
on parental death, but those data also fail to support a derivation
from the theory of grief work that emphasizes memories. Apparently
the fact that most diarists had not been living for some time with a
parent who died means that a substantial amount of disconnecting
had already occurred before the parent died (cf. Bowlby, 1980,
p. 175, on significance of coresidence in grief over death of parent).
Mary Richardson Walker, one of the diarists who was not living with
a parent who died, certainly seemed to have a sense of previous
disconnecting. In a statement previously quoted in Chapter 5, she
seems to have had the disconnecting in mind when she expressed
surprise at how much capacity she still had to feel the loss of her
mother.

* * * * * * *

". . . . I had as I thought already buried my friends so that I imagined I
should hardly reallize [sic] their death when it should occur, but I find this is
not the case. I feel very sensibly the loss of my mother. . . ."

Diary of Mary Richardson Walker (1963, p. 270), entry of July 18, 1844.

* * * * * * *

That connections might have been much stronger and the relationship of diarist age to grief different if the diarists had been living
with a parent at the time the parent died is suggested by the following passage from the diary of Archibald L. Gillies. At the time of the
entry, Gillies was teaching in a nearby community, returning to his

family home as he had on many previous weekends. This return was, however, his first since his mother's death.

* * * * * * *

"Teaching school. Walked out home. . . . This is the first time that I went home and had no friendly greeting from the best friend I ever had on earth. When in former times I would go home on Friday evenings a greeting would await me from her. [W]ith extended hand would she meet me and her question would be 'Well Archie how have you got along this week?' and would then question me on things of importance. How happy would I be. . . . How delightful, how beatific was it to enter upon a week's work knowing that at the end there would be a greeting like this. Certainly it was something to work hard for, even if only to know that mother took such a delight in the good done not only by we her family but by everyone. . . . No more shall the warm greeting meet us on our return from our daily work; no more shall that silver and angelic voice be heard as she gave advice. . . ; no more shall we in company with our beloved mother tread the paths of this world side by side; no more shall we . . . take our walk up the maple lane. . . ."

Diary of Archibald L. Gillies, unpublished manuscript, Archives of Ontario, entry of April 28, 1893, 19 days after his mother's death.

* * * * * * *

Spouse Deaths

For spouses, a derivation from the theory of grief work that focuses on memories would lead to the expectation that the longer the marriage the greater would be the diarist's grief over death of spouse. In the following diary excerpt, which also appeared in Chapter 2, Dustin G. Cheever referred to the many reminders of his wife, who had been dead a bit over a year. That sort of entry seems reasonable to expect, given the theory's emphasis on the importance of memory in grief.

* * * * * * *

". . . How many things occur day by day to remind me of the irreparable loss of her that was dearer to me than all the world beside. Twenty-one years ago this evening we were united in the Holy Bonds of Matrimony & for twenty long years enjoyed each others society, as happy a married couple as ever lived on this wicked earth, but alas how changed is all now, she gone home to rest while I lonely & sad plod along the journey of life."

Diary of Dustin G. Cheever, unpublished manuscript, State Historical Society of Wisconsin, entry of January 4, 1874, a year and three days after the death of his wife, who died close to the couple's twentieth wedding anniversary.

* * * * * * *

For all spouse deaths, the duration of marriage in the 17 cases where it can be determined ranged from 2 years to 55 years. These 17 cases were divided into a group of eight with shorter marriages (10 years or less) and a group of nine with longer marriages (17 years or more). In eight of the first 10 months following loss, grief was present more often for those with shorter marriages; for the other two months of the first 10, grief was present as often for one group as for the other. Seventeen of the remaining 26 months of the first three years of bereavement had variability in grief, so a direction of relationship could be determined. In 14 of these 17, grief was present in proportionately more cases for the diarists with longer marriages. Thus, in the short run (the first 10 months of bereavement), the data run counter to the prediction of the theory of grief work, but in the long run they tend to support it. This pattern is congruent with the findings of Sanders (1980-1981) on the relationship of widow and widower age to early and subsequent grieving.

Conclusions about Duration of Relationship

Although duration-of-relationship predictions from the theory of grief work do not receive strong support, the patterning of the findings is interesting and plausible. The data seem most clearly to run counter to the prediction that longer relations would lead to more grief in the case of sibling deaths (most or all of which occurred while diarist and sibling were not living together), parent deaths (only two parents died while living with a diarist) and deaths of noncoresident offspring. The data also run counter to the prediction from the theory of grief work in the short run for spouses (all but two of whom were living together, and those two had been separated only a short time). But in the long run the theory of grief work receives support from the data on grief over spouse death. The factor that seems to control the applicability of the theory of grief work is coresidence. The data on relationships that were largely or entirely noncoresident at the time of death seem to indicate that when people no longer live together, they begin to disconnect behavior patterns and memories from one another. For deaths of siblings, parents, and noncoresident offspring, apparently the longer the relationship the longer diarist and deceased had been separated.

Then, when the death occurred, there was less grief for longer relationships because the diarist had had more time to become disconnected from the decedent.

The fact that even with coresidence, shorter marriages led to greater grief during the months immediately following the loss can be explained in several ways. One can remain loyal to the theory of grief work and argue that to spouses of shorter duration one has attached more hopes. The potential of the other person and of the relationship remains great and dreams numerous and positive. Then the initially stronger grief for a recently acquired spouse could be understood as grief over broken hopes. If that were so, it would appear that the grief work dealing with loss of hope is carried out more rapidly than the grief work dealing with memories and behavior patterns.

However, most diary accounts of reactions to death in comparatively new close relationships, such as the loss of a young child or a comparatively new spouse, do not contain references to hopes in the first month of grief. In fact, only one diary of a newly bereaved parent grieving for a young child and one diary of a newly bereaved widow grieving for a husband recently married seem to mention lost hope.

* * * * * * *

"This day hath the cold messenger of death entered our dwelling! (solemn thought) and snatched away Dear Son!. . . . This blooming flower must be niped [sic] in the bud, and lay'd away for the worms to devor [sic]. . . ."

Diary of Sally Squire, unpublished manuscript, New Public Library, entry of July 8, 1815.

* * *

"My friend was kind, affectionate, amiable, pleasing & one of the best of husbands. Our attachment was sincere and daily strengthened. We lived a little moment of happiness, but alas death . . . clamp'd the bright picture youth ever forms & tinged my future days with gloom. . . ."

Diary of Sophia Sewell Wood, unpublished manuscript, Sterling Memorial Library, Yale University, entry of March 13, 1810.

* * * * * * *

For Squire and Wood the references to a blooming flower nipped in the bud and to the end of an attachment "daily strengthened" and of "the bright picture youth ever forms" seem to express loss of hope. So there is a hint, but only a hint, that for bereaved spouses and for parents who had lost a young child, part of their grief work was to come to terms with a loss of hope.

It may be, alternatively, that deaths of recently married spouses were experienced by younger people, and that the pattern of data for marital relationships reflects the grief dynamics of younger persons. Older diarists expressed less grief during all 12 months in the first year following a death and in 17 of the 21 months with variability in grief in the second and third years following a death. The age difference could represent several factors. Younger people may have been grieving for their own mortality as well as for the person who had died. They might not yet have learned as much as older people about emotional control (see the next chapter). Older people might have expected losses and been more prepared for them (cf. Parkes, 1981, on the impact of anticipation of loss on subsequent bereavement in younger persons). Thus, the finding that in the early months of bereavement there was more grief for spouses of shorter duration may mean that one initially grieves not only for one's spouse but for one's own mortality, that one is still learning how to control one's emotions, or that the initial grief of older persons is muted by previous preparation for a specific loss or for loss in general. The data of the present study are not useful for differentiating among these alternative possibilities. At any rate, factors associated with diarist age are plausible in explaining the patterning of grief early in bereavement. But considerations of age and hope are not mutually exclusive. Hope may have been stronger and clearer among younger diarists, who had relatively little sense of personal mortality, who had not come to expect losses, and whose hopes blocked some rudimentary emotional preparation for a possible death.

For the quintessential long-term coresidential relationship, marriage, survivors would often be living in proximity to many reminders of the deceased. Moreover, many thoughts and many things heard and seen away from home would be reminders of the deceased. Thus, the data showing that in the long run there is an association of marital duration and grief are consistent with analyses presented throughout this book on the importance of reminders in grief. It was argued in Chapter 4 that reminders have a crucial role in the relationship of anticipation of a loss to subsequent grief, and reminders are important, as the next chapter indicates, in emotional control.

The finding that duration of marriage is associated with grieving runs counter to the presumption that everyone feels the same dreadful feelings over a given kind of loss. The data presented here imply that in the long run people who had longer-term marriages felt worse, provided there had been more or less continuous coresidence. The implication for widows and widowers is that the burden of widowhood is greater on the average after longer marriages. Consistent with that speculation is a report by Rees (1971) that the longer the marriage duration (at least up to 40 years) the more likely a widowed person is to report a sense of the deceased spouse's presence. Rees' data could mean that older patients (Rees was reporting on medical patients) are more willing to admit to experiences that could be labeled hallucinatory. However, the fact that marital duration has an effect in the diary data makes it more plausible that the longer one lives with another the more one's physical environment and thoughts lead to thoughts of the dead spouse so vivid that the spouse seems to be present. Similarly, Weiss, (1975, pp. 62-63) speculated that in divorce there is less upset if the marriage has lasted only a year or two.

The patterning of data on relationship duration and grief is open to alternative interpretation. When the deceased and the bereaved have lived together, the theory of grief work seems to give ambiguous predictions for the early months of grief because hope and memory are counterpoised. At that time, hopes tend to be highest when memories and behavior patterns are not well linked to a person, and hopes may be much less significant when there are heavy linkages of memories and behavior patterns to a person. One can assume that the data on grief for children who were living with a diarist provide an inadequate long-run test of the prediction of the theory of grief work for relationship duration when deceased was living with bereaved. Four to five years might not be a long enough relationship. Thus, only the data on spouses provide an adequate long-run test. The spouse data indicate that in the long run coresidential relationships seem associated with greater grief the longer the relationship. This is what one would expect from an analysis of grief work that emphasized the importance of memories. The reasoning here is, of course, speculative and demands further empirical testing, but the diary data can be accounted for by the counterpoising of hope and memories, the decline of hope as memories build up, and the more rapid completion or near-completion of work on shattered hopes than of work on memories of a person now dead.

9

Controlling Grief

"Earlier this morning I began to be quite melancholy and to feel very lone-some (on Sundays I am more inclined that way). I wanted so much to have someone to talk to or, at the very least, some human being to look at. But Guri and all her family had gone to Sorland's. So I sat in the rocking chair and thought of Vilhelm and wished fervently I might become bright and cheerful again, and was willing to do everything I could to that end. It was really shameful of me to be in such a mood. I realized, too, when I thought of Vilhelm, how good God is to us, and how well off we are. And little by little I became happy and light of heart, and felt only gratitude for all the goodness I have enjoyed, and was distressed to think I had so easily let my mind stray, I, who have so much to rejoice and thank God for and who nevertheless felt upset and in low spirits because I was a little lonely — because Vilhelm was not here."

Diary of Elisabeth Koren (1955, pp. 289-290). Entry of July 30, 1854. She had left her family behind in order to emigrate to the United States with her husband, Vilhelm, a pastor. At the time of this entry her husband was preaching in another community.

* * * * * * *

Diarist Interest in Emotional Control

The self-control of grief is not necessarily desirable and may be a source of problems. In fact, the literature on grief considers the over-controlled bereaved person to be in serious difficulty (see, for example, Bowlby, 1980; Gorer, 1967; Paul & Grosser, 1965). Yet a number of diarists sought to control their grief; none expressed a desire for catharsis of grief, to vent reined-in emotion. Only one diarist seemed to be trying to express strong feelings that she had not been expressing, and also seemed to be trying to force an expression of grief stronger than her internal feelings. Why did the diarists who wrote about emotional limitation or emotional expression give limitation of grief a higher priority than expression? Were they not risking the deleterious effects of pathological overcontrol? Conceivably, anybody who kept a diary may have been expressing grief adequately, but many of the diarists who wrote of a loss expressed virtually no grief in their diary entries. As reported in Chapter 6, diarists expressed grief in only 14.7% of the entries during the first month following a death and in fewer than one percent of the entries during most months of the second and third years following a death. Considering the small proportion of entries with grief, if diary writing allowed a diarist to express grief sufficiently, it took relatively few entries to do it. It is certainly possible, given the small proportion of entries with detectable evidence of grief, that diary writing did not allow for substantial expression of the grief that may have been bottled up. Perhaps grief was expressed in conversation, reverie, participation in a funeral, and performance of other mourning rituals. However, the factors that motivated control of grief in diary writing may have operated in conversation, reverie, funerals and other mourning rituals.

If self-control of grief is risky, perhaps the diarists who were explicit about seeking control were the ones who were more expressive of grief; they expressed it sufficiently and had only to fear an excess. There is some hint of that possibility in the diary data. It can be seen in Table 9.1 that diarists who expressed an interest in emotional control expressed grief in an atypically large number of entries for the first two months following a death. The difference is not large, but it certainly seems to indicate that diarists interested in emotional control were not people who suppressed all feelings. These diarists may, in fact, have been attempting to control feelings that they feared were in danger of excessive expression. Of course, the diarists interested in emotional control might have written more about emotional matters without being different from other diarists in actual feelings. They might even have been expressing their grief authentically, whereas other diarists were controlling by minimizing

Table 9.1. Interest in Grief and Emotional Control: Proportions of Entries with Grief

| Month | Deaths | | Separations | |
	Diarists Interested in Control	All Diarists Combined	Diarists Interested in Control	All Diarists Combined
1	.183	.147	.055	.056
2	.115	.060	.027	.025
3	.044	.040	.015	.021
4	.000	.016	.029	.022
5	.020	.010	.024	.017
6	.014	.017	.019	.017

the significance of their grief. It is not possible, with the diary data, to decide whether the diarists who wrote of controlling emotion were feeling different feelings from the diarists who did not write of controlling. However, an examination of what diarists who wrote about control said about their emotions, about their needs to control, and about the ways they attempted to control provides an interesting perspective on emotional control in grief.

Motives for Control of Grief

Why might a diarist have been interested in controlling grief? There are myriad possibilities. Among the most obvious are that feelings were dreadfully painful; the feelings may have made a diarist want to do things that seemed sinful or could be hurtful to others; and a diarist might have feared insanity if grief were uncontrolled. Grief may have interfered with valued activities, and may have seemed to raise questions about acceptance of God's will. Men might typically have felt unmanly if too upset (see Faragher's, 1979, chaps. 4 & 5, analysis of gender differences in emotionality among nineteenth-century pioneers in the United States).

Some of the 13 diarists who were most explicitly interested in emotional control gave reasons for their interest. Whether these were the only reasons or the "real" reasons (reasons they would have admitted if they were being deeply introspective and attempting to be totally honest with themselves) cannot be determined, but the reasons are still interesting. The two most common reasons were to deal with problems that arose or intensified as a result of the death and to maintain or establish a comfortable relationship with God.

One example of a diarist who sought control in order to deal with or solve problems arising from a loss is Mrs. William B. Dodd (her file at the Minnesota Historical Society does not give her own first and middle name or her maiden name). Her husband was killed in the so-called Sioux War in Minnesota in 1862, and she had problems stemming from government requisitioning of produce grown on her farm, from two young children, and from farm work that previously had been done or managed by her husband. In the early days of her bereavement, Mrs. Dodd wrote: "Let my prayer be not that [my daughter] may be rich, beautiful or great in the world's eyes, but that she may be among the meek and lowly who shall be elevated in the Kingdom of God. And I must be the fit mother of such an one. To what perfection must I not strive to attain? Let no hasty or indecent actions mar my conduct." (Unpublished diary, Minnesota Historical Society, entry of Saturday, September 6, 1862).

The next day Mrs. Dodd wrote that "Dr. Daniels stopped in today and talked of the last hours of my husband. I must not live in the past. My whole thought must be of my present duty. To improve myself in mind in heart and manners. To cultivate in my children habits of neatness, order and diligence." Clearly, for Mrs. Dodd, the problems of raising children without help could be seen as a source of need for control of her grief, though one might also argue that parenting and other concerns were an excuse to defend against a too painful grief.

The other frequently mentioned motive for emotional control seems to be a need to have what the diarist considered the proper relationship with God. Some bereaved diarists seemed to fear that their intense grief might offend God, perhaps because it might indicate that the lost person was in some sense a worshipped god. Some diarists may have feared the consequences of being angry with God or of offending God by questioning His wisdom or beneficence. Or perhaps the concerns were more earthly—a fear of maintaining improper religious decorum and of damaging relations with co-religionists. As one example of religious motivation for controlling grief, consider the following, written by Sally Squire 27 days after the death of her two-year-old son.

* * * * * * *

"Returned from a visit, but alass! no darling Son to wellcome my safe arrival. I look through my rooms but all is gloomy & silent! Where is the voice that used to cheer this once happy dwelling? Ah, it is silent in death!. . . . God is now saying . . . if I love God why do I mourn that his will is done? because of my wicked heart. . . ." Unpublished manuscript, New York Public Library, entry of August 4, 1815. The next entry seems to indicate that Squire believed that her continuing grief had moved God to withhold spiritual peace from her.

"One month hath elapsed and I have not committed pen to paper because my sins appear so dreadful exposed to the naked eye! . . . I am almost ready to despair and say there is no sorrow equal to my sorrow. I had the reviving thought when I saw my only Son expire that God would put no more upon me than I could bear, but I little thought in the deep anguish of my heart that he would withdraw the comforts of his grace! I want words to paint the anxiety of my mind!" Entry of September 4, 1815. In an entry written three months later her grief seems to have diminished and her relation with her God to have become more comfortable:

"O! the wonderfull condescension of God . . . that he should permit me to see the vanity of placing my affections upon this unsatisfying world but cal'd my wandering thoughts home to thee. . . ." Entry of December 14, 1815.

* * * * * * *

Of course, the motives people avowed may simply have been rationalizations covering unacceptable motives for control or offering explanations for the inexplicable. But a case can be made for the incompatibility of strong grief with almost any activity. So even if control of grief can only be accomplished over short periods of time, it still might be useful.

Means of Controlling Grief

The motives for controlling emotions are not entirely distinct from the means of controlling them. In fact, the reasons diarists gave probably indicate something about their values and their normal lines of thinking. If, for example, they were concerned about their relation with God, it may be religious acts that helped them to control. If they were concerned about dealing with some practical problem arising from the loss, working on the problem may have been a way of distancing the feelings of loss. From another perspective, the means of emotional control people chose may have been in operation at the time they justified its use, so they might have inferred or rationalized their stated reasons for controlling emotions in terms linked to the control mechanism. For example, if a diarist controlled emotion through preoccupation with religious thoughts or through self-instruction in the form of prayer, he or she might have concluded that emotion was being controlled in order to establish a proper relationship with God. Reasons for controlling grief and statements about how the diarist was trying to control it tend to come in the same diary entries and may even be inferable from the same sentence. Despite the blending in the data of the two analytically separable categories, motives and means, it may be useful to retain a separation in writing about grief.

The diarists seem to have used four major methods of controlling emotions: (1) acting inconsistently with feelings, (2) self-instruction to behave in a controlled fashion, (3) avoiding reminders of the loss, and (4) cognitive minimizing of the loss. These means of control are generally congruent with contemporary behavior modification approaches to self-control (e.g., Mahoney & Thoresen, 1974). Some diarists used several different means. The four means of dealing with emotion may have been employed in a variety of emotional situations, not merely for grief, so the dynamics of control in grief may tell something about the dynamics of emotional control in the face of anger, lust, fear, and other emotions that people may have wanted to control.

Acting Inconsistently with Feelings

Some diarists stated very clearly that they tried to deal with feelings arising from a loss by acting as though things were not so bad. Some said that they did this in order not to burden others with their grief, others because it helped them feel better. One example of a diarist who tried to act inconsistently with feelings is a woman whose parents died when she was young (the second parent dying when she was 17) and who was separated from her siblings for long periods after the first parental death. In the entry quoted here, she was, at age 21, parting with her sister Hexa for what was anticipated to be at least one year.

* * * * * * *

"Early this morning we saw Hexa off on the steamer for Halden. We set out quite cheerily with the hat box between us. We are becoming accustomed to partings and travel and have learned to press back the pain in our hearts behind a smooth exterior. . . . We wave a cheery farewell, though not within our hearts."

Diary of Linka Keyser (1952, p. 101), entry of August 6, 1850. Halden is in Norway. The diarist emigrated to the United States in 1851.

* * * * * * *

This quote from the diary of Linka Keyser suggests that the control of emotions through putting on a front may be a learned process. If that can be generalized, it would suggest that one may struggle for emotional control more, and be more self-conscious about it, during the early losses of one's life. In fact, the average age at which diarists first mentioned emotional control to deal with a separation or death was 37.64 years of age (for 11 losses), whereas the average age at onset of loss for all deaths and separations in which emotional control is not clearly mentioned in a diary entry was 45.62 (for 298 losses). Diarists expressing an interest in emotional control were, on the average, eight years younger, which supports the notion that the struggle for emotional control may be more salient in younger persons, before emotional control skills are well enough learned. The quote from the Keyser diary may even imply that early losses lead to more grief, in part because there is less ability to control the most painful feelings. The question of age differences in grief feelings is addressed more fully in the last section of this chapter. Linka Keyser's statement also indicates that the control of emotions through inconsistent action was not entirely effective for her. What did she feel within her heart? Perhaps less pain than she would have felt without her happy exterior, but perhaps not.

Psychological studies indicate that under some circumstances people are pushed in the direction of matching their actual feelings with their overt expressions of feeling (see, for example, Lanzetta, Cartwright-Smith, & Kleck, 1976). So even if Linka Keyser's happy exterior failed to change her feelings, perhaps for other bereaved people a happy exterior might alter feelings at least temporarily. The quote further on in this chapter from Ada James may indicate more effective emotional control through putting on a happy exterior, but the example is not entirely convincing because James seems, in one sentence, to have attributed the effective control more to keeping busy than to appearing happy.

Self-Instruction

Some diarists seem to have controlled their feelings of grief or to have tried to control them through self-instruction, either in the form of prayer or through a wish or resolution. Elisabeth Koren, in the passage quoted at the beginning of this chapter, seems to have been using wishes as self-instruction. In another example, a month after her mother died hundreds of miles away in Michigan, Emily Hawley Gillespie wrote the following poem:

* * * * * * *

How is Father to night;
I hope he is all right.
Pleasant be all his dreams,
Sweet his sleep, as it seems.
This world is not so sad a world
If ever happy we try to make it.
May we retire to night all sins forgiven
Begin the morrow with hopes all bright,
Forget as it were the sadness of the past
True happiness can our sorrows out last.

Diary of Emily Hawley Gillespie. Unpublished transcript, State Historical Society of Iowa, Iowa City. Entry of August 18, 1882.

* * * * * * *

One could make a case that she was trying to limit her grief over her mother's death through avoiding reference to her mother and through worrying about her father's well-being. And, in fact, her self-instruction in that poem seems to have been to forget the sadness of the past. Whether she meant that one can make the world less sad by trying to make others and oneself happy or that one can be happier if one tries to think about happy things is not clear. But it is clear that she saw forgetting as potentially of use.

Prayer may also be self-instruction. Some prayers that diarists entered in their diaries listed tasks that had to be done; God was asked to help the diarist with these tasks, including dealing with grief. The prayer of Mrs. William B. Dodd quoted earlier in this chapter is an example; here are two others:

* * * * * * *

"Alone! . . . My wife dead, my child an alien to my home! God give me strength to bear and submit."

Diary of Martin W. Phillips (1909, p. 480), entry of June 2, 1862. His wife had died in January, 1862.

* * *

"Jacob is dead. Tears blind my eyes as I write. Oh my how sick he was, but now he is at rest, my little Darling Jacob. Hope to meet you in heaven. God help me to bear my sorrow. . . ."

Diary of Sophia Lovick. Unpublished diary loaned by Rosalie Norem. Entry of August 25, 1897. Jacob was Sophia Lovick's infant son.

* * * * * * *

Both Phillips and Lovick, by asking God for the strength to bear their sorrow, seem to be telling themselves that they must live with their sorrow. They were in that sense setting goals for themselves. Self-instruction to control feelings might often have been a hidden component of any relationship with God during grief. To the extent that a diarist believed that God knew inner feelings, and to the extent that religious beliefs demanded acceptance of God's will, people might have thought that feelings that seemed to question God's wisdom had to be controlled. Linka Keyser was among several diarists with a strong religious orientation who expressed a sense of the importance of controlling feelings that could seem to question God's wisdom. ". . . How glad I am that I have arrived at a point these last days when I seem not to be false if I say: 'I thank Thee, O God, that Thou didst take Sister unto Thyself'" (Keyser, 1952, p. 238, entry of September 1, 1853). Until she could achieve enough acceptance of her sister's death to thank God, she might have been experiencing pressure from her religious convictions to control the feelings that seemed somehow to accuse God of an unfair or otherwise inappropriate act. Moreover, as this quote seems to indicate, the mere appearance of acceptance was insufficient when dealing with God. Because honesty with oneself was so important in spiritual life or because one could never deceive God, the most religiously observant diarists seemed to feel strong pressure to control inner thoughts and feelings, not merely to achieve the semblance of control.

Diary writing itself can be seen as a form of self-instruction. As one writes about what has happened and how one feels, one is defining the situation and one's reactions. The act of defining may be seen as an act of controlling, delimiting, and shaping one's emotional expression. One may also be controlling emotions through distracting oneself by composing one's sentences, by distancing events enough in one's thoughts so that one can write about them, and by the physical act of writing.

Self-instruction, or the making of plans, has been demonstrated repeatedly in psychological research to be effective in self-control (see, for example, Kendall & Hollon, 1979; Meichenbaum & Goodman, 1979; Mischel, 1979; Mischel & Patterson, 1976). It should come as no surprise that many diarists used self-instruction and planning in self-control. The diarists, like other people in the nineteenth century, often used the Bible and other religious writings as guides to how to behave (cf. Douglas, 1977, chap. 6). Although nineteenth-century religion also involved spiritual acts and feelings, social interaction, entertainment, plea making, and other things, the control element seems quite commonly to have been present.

Avoiding Reminders of the Lost

There is cross-cultural evidence that avoiding reminders of a deceased spouse helps to facilitate remarriage (Rosenblatt, Walsh, and Jackson, 1976, chap. 4), and there is substantial anecdotal evidence from contemporary European and North American society that many bereaved people are motivated to distance or to avoid painful reminders (Bowlby, 1980; DeVaul, Zisook, & Faschingbauer, 1979; Silverman & Silverman, 1979). One could argue, in fact, that avoidance of stimuli is a means of control for many different emotions (Rosenblatt & Titus, 1976; Rosenblatt, Walsh & Jackson, 1976) and the control mechanism most commonly used. Among the diarists in the sample, it was the most often discussed mode of control. No diarist seemed to eliminate all reminders of the lost person; in modern clinical work, elimination of reminders of the deceased is sometimes seen as a source or correlate of pathological grieving (Gauthier & Marshall, 1977). But many diarists worked at least some of the time at distancing, ignoring, or eliminating reminders of a lost person. Keeping busy is one way to do this. Several diarists, including Mrs. William B. Dodd in a passage quoted earlier in this chapter, wrote about keeping busy as a means of coping with their feelings resulting from a loss. In the following passage, Ada James praised the busy life.

* * * * * * *

"Since I last wrote in my diary how very much has happened. This year has been sad, so sad. — Beulah is in Boston and my other sister Annie — in heaven. . . . Life at present does look *so* sad, but my religion is to *try* to be happy, at least to seem so and try to make others happy. I am happy because I am busy, and that is everythink [sic], but how deeply do I feel at times when I am not on my guard. . . ."

Diary of Ada James. Unpublished manuscript, State Historical Society of Wisconsin, Madison. Entry of March 10, 1898. (Note: This diary was not part of the sample used in data tabulations, but it is cited here because of its relevance.)

* * * * * * *

Keeping busy was not the only way to avoid reminders of the lost person (cf. Glick, Weiss, & Parkes, 1974, p. 139); some diarists used sleep to avoid reminders.

* * * * * * *

"I am a little homesick tonight. I am thinking of Mollie dear! and of the many dear friends of the past. My life is not what I pictured it a year ago. My airy castles have tumbled and I feel *so* far away. The rain is falling in torrents, thunder peals and lightnings flash. The wind moans thro these tall trees a requiem to joy, but there, Mollie, yours not to be blue. I'll hie me to bed and forget in slumber all that is calculated to make me sad. Good-night! my Journal."

Diary of Mollie Dorsey Sanford (1959, p. 38), entry of June 23, 1857.

* * *

"I have meandered here & there, have engaged in exciting business away away [sic] from home and all those thousands of reminders there of my irreparable loss, hoping that time would assuage in some small degree the sorrow of soul, but it is all of no avail to night. The hurt bleeds & the tears flow. I try not to murmur or complain. Heaven is just. God is merciful & loving & doeth all things well, does them for our good & his glory and our great loss is the dear ones eternal gain. Heaven help us to admire it all. . . . I lay down the pen & if possible will try & seek repose in sleep."

Diary of Dustin G. Cheever. Unpublished manuscript, State Historical Society of Wisconsin, Whitewater Regional Historical Center. Entry of December 31, 1873. Cheever's wife died in January, 1873.

* * * * * * *

Cheever's entry indicates that the avoidance of stimuli to grief was for him by no means a permanent means of dealing with a loss. Feelings returned, though it is hard to know whether they were as intense as they would have been closer to the time of loss. Cheever's entry also indicates his wrestling with questions about God, a common response among the diarists to the death of a loved one, particularly a child or a spouse who was not elderly. In the process of wrestling with God, Cheever also used prayer as self-instruction.

Still other diarists avoided stimuli, as Cheever did, but did so through avoiding thoughts or at least through avoiding writing of the lost person.

* * * * * * *

"I am loosing [sic] control of my feelings so I can't write any more."

Diary of Ada James, unpublished manuscript, State Historical Society of Wisconsin, Madison, entry of November 1, 1896. Her grief was over a recently ended romantic relationship.

* * *

"Were I to sit down & brood over the various circumstances of my late sorrowful bereavement it w^d unfit me for every active duty. My mind w^d dwell on its own personal calamities 'till my health w^d be undermined & all the faculties I possess weakened, & perverted. When my thoughts do fasten on this one point, his sick bed, it produces emotions so powerful as almost to overwhelm me. . . ." (April 13, 1820)

"Just a year tomorrow since my blessed husband preached for the last time in our church. These retrospections are [?] painful. But I don't cherish them. I find it better to keep my mind earnestly engaged with present concerns & duties." (July 8, 1820)

Diary of Susan Mansfield Huntington, unpublished manuscript, Sterling Memorial Library, Yale University. Her husband had died in September, 1819.

* * *

"I do not understand why all at once I can become so sad, or depressed, or whatever I should call it. It starts with a longing for Vilhelm, then everything about me seems so empty: I become rather faint and have to take a little walk and look around. That helps sometimes, especially when I happen to see something beautiful, as when today I saw a new kind of bluebird, with white underbody and light-red breast—that helps. And then when I can, I avoid thinking of Vilhelm (at least when I begin to long for him, you know) or of anyone at home or in Norway. Sometimes it helps to read—when I can persuade myself to pick up a book. This mood is sometimes of long, sometimes of short duration; but I simply cannot understand why it comes so suddenly while I am sitting here in good spirits. If only Vilhelm were home! But tomorrow is Sunday. Perhaps Monday he will come. God grant it! Now I am in good spirits again; but that was not true when I took out my writing case. In the meantime Kari came before I had begun to write and asked if she might bake bread in the oven. So I took a little walk with her. That helped."

Diary of Elisabeth Koren (1955, p. 264), entry of July 8, 1854. (Note: This separation was too short to be included in data tabulations, but it is cited here because of its relevance to emotional control).

* * * * * * *

The three passages quoted here indicate how painful the feelings were that the diarists worked at controlling. The entries just quoted from the diaries of Ada James and Susan Mansfield Huntington suggest that diaries and diary keeping were at times stimuli to that pain. This adds credence to the notion that although diaries may have been used by some people for emotional self-expression, others may have avoided writing of a loss because of the painful emotions the writing set off. Elisabeth Koren said she used walks, the search for beautiful things, reading, and social interaction (but not diary writing) to help her avoid thinking of her absent husband and the relatives and friends she left behind in Norway.

The use of distraction to control grief may be easier if one has relatively rich social relationships. The literature on grief commonly treats social isolation as a symptom of poor grief work, but it may be that the social isolation is a *cause* of poor (or at least relatively slow) grief work. The fact that people who live alone tend to be more depressed a year after the death of a spouse (Bornstein, Clayton, Halikas, Maurice, & Robins, 1973; Clayton, 1975) may in part be due to their lack of social interactions to distract them from their grief.

If social interactions can reduce the pain of grief, why would people choose to be socially isolated? For some people it may not be a matter of choice (cf. Lopata, 1973, pp. 266-270), but others clearly have the opportunity for considerable social contact. Perhaps, for some people with such opportunities, encounters with others early in bereavement may be quite painful (cf. DeVaul, Zisook, & Faschingbauer, 1979). Consider the following quote from the diary of Sophia Sewell Wood.

* * * * * * *

". . . every scene & every face before recognized served only to embitter my disappointment in life & the retrospect of a few short months when gayety & happiness were mine. . . ."

Diary of Sophia Sewell Wood, unpublished manuscript. Sterling Memorial Library, Yale University, entry of March 10, 1809, six days after her husband's death.

* * * * * * *

For Wood, avoiding people might have led to avoiding some pain. For people like her there might be a temptation to avoid and to continue the avoidance of others. However, if contacts persist beyond the early, most painful encounters, perhaps because of feelings of social obligation or because patterns of interactions with kin, friends, and neighbors are too well established to terminate, the long-run effect might be less pain. In other words, the early interactions after a very bereaving loss might be so painful as to motivate one to isolate oneself from others, but people who are strongly pressured to maintain interaction may in the long run experience less severe grief.

Finally, the value of avoiding reminders of the lost in the control of grief is shown in first returns to places that were significant in one's relationship with the lost. For a substantial number of diarists, this first return had a jarring emotional impact, bringing them grief more intense, more nearly overwhelming than they had experienced immediately before the return. A passage expressing such reactions has already been quoted in this chapter from the diary of Sally Squire ("Returned from a visit. . . .") and another, from the diary of William Brisbane, can be read in the next section of this chapter ("I made much effort yesterday. . . ."). See also the quote in the next chapter from the diary of Henry Scadding (". . . In administering the sacramental cup. . . ."). Returnings were common in part because many diarists left home temporarily after the death of a coresident. The frequency of temporary change of residence following a loss gives some sense of how painful reminders of a lost person might have been (cf. Parkes, 1972, p. 88). The frequency of strong emotional reactions on first returning to that home, or to some other significant place, indicates that effective grief work requires one to neutralize somehow the pain potential of familiar settings and to somehow change the meaning of familiar stimuli. Freud argued that this is the key to grief work.

For the person who is not forewarned of the pain of first returnings, a first returning can be one of those instances where a surge of grief comes up unexpectedly, after the person has thought grief had abated. The significance of first returnings supports arguments made in Chapter 5 about the psychological impact on survivors of having dying relatives cared for in hospitals, rather than at home. With hospitalization, the stimuli at home are not so strongly associated with the terminal illness—although the hospital is, which may make survivors very unhappy in a hospital. With the home environment not so heavily charged with painful reminders, learning to live with the loss may be easier.

Cognitive Minimizing of the Loss

The fourth major kind of mechanism for control of grief is the cognitive minimizing of loss, determining that what has happened somehow is not so bad after all. Minimizing involves a redefinition of the situation as one not solely of loss or not a loss at all. Redefinition is one of the most commonly used cognitive mechanisms of emotional control, if one can judge from its significance in the literature on emotional control in the face of anxiety- or fear-provoking situations (e.g., Koriat, Melkman, Averill, & Lazarus, 1972; Lazarus, 1975).

Diarists in the sample minimized their losses in several ways. One was to set expectations low, so that almost any outcome would be better than what was expected. The following passage from the diary of Thomas Edmonds expresses eloquently this way of making the best of experiences.

* * * * * * *

"Yes! alone I am. . . . Happiness consists not so much in having a good deal to enjoy, as in the faculty to be contented with a little. . . ."

Diary of Thomas Edmonds. Unpublished manuscript, Huntington Library. Entry of May 16, 1844. His wife was away; his daughter-in-law (the widow of his recently deceased son) and grandchild had moved away a month before.

* * * * * * *

Another way diarists minimized loss was to decide that the lost person was much better off than if still with the diarist. There was some of that in the passages quoted earlier in this chapter from the diaries of Sophia Lovick and Dustin Cheever. The following passage from the diary of William Brisbane, written on the day his teenaged son Bentley died, seems to contain an attempt to minimize loss through a claim that the deceased is well off dead because his spirit "is with Jesus."

* * * * * * *

"And now shall I have a reprising thought? God forbid. I would say to my soul, Peace, be still—and know that the Judge of all the earth must do right. I cannot, I dare not wish him back. His spirit I feel assured is with Jesus. O my Jesus! May I from this hour be always thine, entirely thine!"

Diary of William Brisbane. Unpublished manuscript, State Historical Society of Wisconsin, Madison. Entry of March 22, 1846.

* * * * * * *

By "reprising thought" Brisbane meant something like a wish to have his son back. Brisbane may have been wrestling with God or with his idea of God, and he seems to have been working toward both emotional control and peace with God by instructing himself to accept the death and consider it a good thing because his son was "with Jesus." However, 20 months later, upon returning to the city (Cincinnati) and the very house in which his son died, Brisbane experienced intense grief.

* * * * * * *

"I made much effort yesterday to suppress my feelings, but on going to bed I could no longer bear up under the pressure. I spent a sad, sobbing melancholy night in remembrance of my beloved Bentley who occupied the adjoining chamber

when he died. Oh, how gloomy every thing appears to me, for every thing reminds me of him. . . ."

Diary of William Brisbane, entry of November 8, 1847.
* * * * * * *

Obviously the redefinitions and other devices that Brisbane used in
the hours, days, and months following his son's death were insufficient to prevent strong grief when he was faced again with reminders
of his loss, although there were plenty of intervening entries that
lacked any reference to Bentley. Brisbane's entry of November 8, 1847,
illustrates how important reminders of a deceased person are in producing grief. Bentley had not only died in the house Brisbane was
visiting, but had died there (slowly and in agony) over a period of many
days. So the reminders were strongly associated with the loss. During
the intervening months, Brisbane had stayed away from that house.
The fresh reminders temporarily outweighed whatever coming to
terms with the loss Brisbane had achieved. Minimizing loss through
defining it as the lost person's gain seems, like the other means of
emotional control, only a temporary measure, one insufficient to
prevent grief from reemerging in the face of strong stimuli to grief.

One means a diarist could use for minimizing loss was to deny
somehow that the loss had really occurred. That means was used by
only one diarist, who became a believer in spiritism following the
death of two of his children and his mother. Although Marcus Gunn
was not without other means mentioned here for controlling emotions, on January 27, 1854, approximately a month and a half after
learning of the death of his mother and one of his sons, Gunn wrote
"Oh Lord God Almighty give me some tangible evidence of the immortality of my beloved ones removed from my sight. I *need* it, oh
Lord!!" (Public Archives of Canada, unpublished transcript) Two
days later he was able to write that "I went . . . to a . . . Medium
of correspondence with departed Spirits & saw the phenomena of
Table Motion & had affected responses with my beloved Boys gone.
. . ." Following that first spiritualist contact he developed an elab-
orate program of contact with spirits of the deceased. Details are provided in Chapter 10, in a discussion of family-systems-theory approaches to grief, but it suffices to say here that spiritism seems a
means of minimizing a death or an adjunct to another means of minimizing — believing that the deceased is better off because in heaven.

A final type of minimizing found in the diaries is the decision that the loss has somehow improved the life of the loser. Several diarists said, for example, that God had brought them closer to grace or had educated them through taking the life of a loved one. Some diarists said that a loss, in some cases not even the loss of someone close, led to taking life more seriously. Thomas Dent, a Chicago attorney, wrote the following shortly after the death of a grown daughter, his only child:

* * * * * * *

". . . With what sadness do I think of the death of my dear child; a sadness that brings to memory many mistakes and great imperfection on my part in my career thus far. Small prejudices have sometimes influenced me to my disadvantage. At least, it seems so to me now. I have also failed to speak out at times when I ought to have spoken, & have been too inconsiderate as to what I should say or leave unsaid."

Diary of Thomas Dent, unpublished manuscript, Chicago Historical Society, entry of April 8, 1882.

* * * * * * *

Dent may have been expressing general guilt feelings, but it is clear from other passages that the death of his daughter motivated him to work more diligently and to be more careful in his social relationships. Minimizing by finding good in the bad may not eliminate the bad, but it may alter the balance to make the bad seem not quite so overwhelming.

One phenomenon that could augment feelings of grief rather than control them is sanctification of the lost. Lopata (1975, 1981) has written about husband sanctification in widowhood. She found, for example, that most of the widows in her large sample considered their husbands to have been unusually good men, their marriages above average, and their homes unusually happy. Some widows and widowers among the diarists seemed also to be sanctifying (see, for example, the quote from the diary of Dustin G. Cheever in the previous chapter—"as happy a married couple as ever lived"). Does that mean that some people enhance their pain and grieving rather than control it? Not necessarily. As Lopata (1981) points out, sanctification may keep one away from memories inconsistent with the sanctification. It may also motivate one to distance grief for hopes of good things in the relationship that were never attained. Although people who sanctify may somehow be enhancing grief, they may be controlling it.

Does Emotional Control Work?

Other control mechanisms may have been used by the diarists, and there are undoubtedly many that they did not touch on. One could classify the mechanisms that have been discussed here in a different way. But an overriding question remains, particularly in an age when the popular literature on grief argues that venting of feelings is a good means of avoiding pathological grieving: Does the control help one to live more comfortably or effectively with one's loss?

As several passages quoted earlier in this chapter indicate, trying to control grief or even controlling it effectively now does not guarantee that one will be free of grief later on. Control may provide time to deal with what has to be done immediately. But whether one gets anything more or different in the long run is hard to say. As Dolly Lunt Burge seems to say in the following quotation, grief may change with the passage of time, but if it does not, breaking up the bouts of pain may make life much more tolerable than if they were continuous or seemingly out of one's control.

* * * * * * *

"Six years ago to-day since my dear Samuel left me for a better & brighter world. Ah, the stroke, the bitter, bitter cup. Can I ever forget it? Little did I then think that I should have remained so long separated from him. But this unfaithful heart though it does not forget often puts out of mind these sad memories & it is well that we are thus constituted for the burden of grief that was first upon me I could not have long borne."

Diary of Dolly Lunt Burge (1962, p. 30), entry of September 19, 1849. Samuel was her first husband.

* * * * * * *

Costs of Control

No diarist in the sample seems to have developed pathological grief symptoms. For example, there is no diarist who had a period of insanity or of depression that precluded any productive activity, slept constantly, or suffered from anorexia. As in twentieth-century studies of grief in randomly selected bereaved people (e.g., Clayton, 1982), no diarist seemed to feel pervasively guilty. It may be that such things did happen, but were unrecorded in the diaries or supporting documents, or it may be that diary writing kept diarists from developing pathologies. It is conceivable that all the emotional control mechanisms the diarists used were comparatively short-term, rather than applied constantly over a long period of time, and that it is the latter type of control that produces pathology.

There is a vast literature, including a considerable body of material written for the educated public, on denial and repression in grief. The major point in that literature is that denial and repression are sources of serious problems, including bizarre thinking, failure to come to grips with a new reality, and physical illnesses arising in part from the tension of keeping one's mind away from what is being denied or repressed. No doubt thinking or acting as though a loss has not occurred is associated with serious problems, but one can be too quick to generalize to all people from individuals with serious problems. Judging by the diary data on emotional control, thinking and acting at times as though a loss has not occurred is common and leads to no great problem.

If there were costs of control, the diarists paid them in the area of expectations. A diarist who had grief under control at one time would be startled at how strongly grief surged at a later time (for example, Cheever). It may be in the nature of grief to recur without adequate warning or time to establish expectations. But the problem of upsetting recurrence may be greater in people who work at emotional control, perhaps especially in people who, like the diarists in the sample who wrote about emotional control, are relatively self-aware.

Effects of Repeated Griefs on Control

Many of the losses that led to diarists' writing about control were early losses in the diary, though not necessarily first losses in the life of the diarist. This may mean that losses not worth mentioning or not worth starting a diary to deal with are also losses that do not demand control. And it may mean that one enters novel information about anything one is doing, including controlling emotions, but does not repeat the information when it is no longer novel.

The losses associated with entries mentioning emotional control were generally what most people would consider great losses. The most common was death of a spouse, and the second most common death of a child. The only other types of loss that caused more than one diarist in the sample to write about control were separation from a spouse and separation from a sibling.

One way to understand the process of emotional control is to consider the effects of repeated losses. Do they lead to a lower level of emotion in diary entries? Answering this question is fraught with problems, since a decrease in emotion in entries may reflect any number of processes in addition to learning to modify one's strongest emotional reactions. Repeated losses may eventually lead to a reduction in emotional level of entries simply because a diarist chooses not to enter redundant information. Or a diarist may simply have lost some of the elements of grief present in early losses. For example, a diarist's fear of death or denial that death could happen to close relatives may decrease, or emotion arising from uncertainty about how to behave when bereaved (cf. Rosenblatt, Walsh, & Jackson, 1976, chap. 3) may disappear after several griefs. Despite these alternative interpretations of a possible reduction in grief resulting from previous experience with death, it still seems worthwhile to establish what the phenomena are. If previous experience with loss leads to the learning of emotional control techniques, one would expect that at least in the earliest months of grief the greater the number of previous experiences with loss the less the grief. There is no reason to expect a strong relationship, because control of emotion does not mean abolition of emotion and because there are many unique, emotion-influencing aspects of any specific loss. For each loss experienced by the diarist the number of previous losses recorded in the diary can be determined. That is not a strong measure of past experience with loss, because there may have been many losses not recorded in the available diary volumes, but it is at least a crude indicator of experience with loss. When the data are examined for both deaths and separations, there is less grief in the first two months of bereavement with greater experience of loss. (See Appendix C for statistical details.)

The previous chapter contained a discussion of age and grief, indicating that older diarists grieved less. In fact, one of the commonly reported effects in the contemporary literature on grief (though not all studies find it) is that younger adults or adults with fewer previous bereavements are affected more by a loss than older adults or adults with more previous bereavements (Bornstein & Clayton, 1972; Clayton, 1975; Maddison & Walker, 1967; Parkes, 1972, pp. 128-130; Sanders, 1980-1981, who reported that younger widows and widowers grieved more at first, less later on). Although that may mean, among other things, that first losses produce emotional reactions partly as a result of facing up to one's own mortality, it may also mean that the younger or less experienced bereaved person has not learned how to control emotions. If so, there are two possible interpretations of the effects of previous experience in the diary data. One is that apparently greater grief is simply an external phenomenon; inside, both more and less experienced were feeling the same grief. Alternatively, the people more experienced at control actually were modulating their internal feelings as a result of that control. Whatever they were doing to control was leading them in part to function in the first months of bereavement at a lower level of personal turmoil. In other words, attempts to control feelings may affect actual feelings.

This is written in a era when law and public opinion have been moving to a view that all people are equally human. This book assumes that diarist griefs are important to study because they are like the griefs of all humans, for example, that one person's grief for a spouse or a child is rather like another's. So when diaries are read that differ greatly in verbosity, it seems appropriate to empathize as strongly with the one-line entry of a taciturn person ("Wife died this morning!!") as with the four-page entry of the fluent diarist. Yet it is possible that griefs tend to be stronger or more complex in those who use more words. Either the amount one writes or the richness with which one expresses feelings may influence the intensity or complexity of feelings. This hypothesis may be probed by exploring the context of the statement by a bereaved person that words cannot express his or her emotions. Although such a statement could mean that the person is feeling nothing or is feeling something too vague to describe, it might mean that the person is experiencing strong or complex feelings that he or she has no vocabulary to describe. It might be a sign that vocabulary limitations do not overwhelmingly limit feelings if the people who most often wrote something like "words cannot express what I feel" are those who wrote with the smallest vocabulary. If the people who wrote with the smallest vocabulary claimed most often to have feelings they could not describe, then vocabulary may limit communication more than it does feelings. To explore the possibility that people who wrote that words could not express what they felt were disproportionately those with less education or a smaller active vocabulary, all first entries of loss and all second entries of loss that were made within a month of the loss were scanned for assertions resembling "words cannot express what I feel." No diarist made such an assertion. Diarists at a loss for words might have entered nothing. Perhaps some of the delayed reports of loss were delayed because the diarists were not yet able to express what they felt. Or perhaps the diarists generally believed that they would be able to decode their own statements and recall what they felt, even though the diary statements were not clear expressions of feelings. At any rate, there is no evidence that people who wrote simply or briefly were more inclined to say that words could not express their feelings. The hypothesis remains (though obviously in need of additional probing) that people who write less or with smaller vocabularies feel grief with less intensity or complexity.

People may delimit their emotional expression by delimiting their words, so the person of fewer words may be aware of less emotion. That is, not sensing oneself expressing grief through the written word may lead one to feel less grief. From a slightly different angle, it may be, as diarists who instructed themselves not to be self-pitying seem to have believed, that the expression of grief leads to a snowballing of grief. The more one expresses, the more one feels, which leads to more expression, which leads to more feeling, etc. One mechanism in the snowballing could be that as one records more details of one's loss and describes any given aspect of the loss with more eloquence, one senses and makes more salient feelings that were before only present in the shadows of one's awareness. Another mechanism has to do with memory. The more words one has for talking about a loss, and hence the wider the range of thinking one engages in with regard to it, the more memories one evokes and the greater is the sense of loss. Thus, a case can be made for the association of verbal fluency and grief.

It is still an open question whether everyone can curtail grief effectively. Case studies indicate that for some people the attempt to avoid dealing with or expressing grief leads to serious personal difficulties that cannot be overcome until the grief is dealt with (see, for example, Paul & Grosser, 1965). Yet there may be people who successfully curtail griefs. If so, one mechanism for curtailment may simply be the limitation of expression of grief. Thus, the person who writes little of grief may actually experience less grief, while the person who uses rich vocabulary and many words to deal with the grief may create a more intense grief.

A related issue is the grief of children or the mentally retarded. Again the issue may not be resolvable, at this time, with empirical testing. But it may be worth considering whether the grief of those with fewer words to deal with a loss is actually as great as the grief of those with more words. One can certainly cite cases of people who, as children, lost a parent and experienced grief with profound intensity then or later. Yet it is conceivable that on the average the losses experienced by children involve less grief than those experienced by adults. Also, the grief that some adults feel later for a parent lost in childhood may represent a search for understanding that never existed, because the child lacked words for thought and communication, or an attempt to come to terms with an adult problem rather than with a problem that has survived since childhood (Johnson & Rosenblatt, 1981). It may, for example, represent either a search for feelings the adult assumes the child must have had or a search for meanings and understandings demanded by personal principles established in maturity, such as: one must make sense of one's childhood and of serious early losses.

A retarded person's grief may be felt with great intensity, but it may be less than that of someone with a rich vocabulary. The vocabulary deficiency may make it impossible ever to compare the grief of a seriously retarded person with the grief of a more normal person. It is certainly possible that a deficient vocabulary does not mute grief but alters it (along routes closed to people with substantial vocabularies) or enlarges it (because lacking words to give understanding adds to the pain). But if one can assess the grief indirectly, for example, through disruption of daily routine or through depressed affect, it may be that people—such as children and the retarded—with smaller vocabularies grieve less.

Finally, the mechanism for stirring up memory may be emotional as well as cognitive (Bower, 1981; Isen, Shalker, Clark, & Karp, 1978). A mood may call forth many associated memories. Thus, people who are more aware of feelings other than grief may experience more grief as a result of processes instigated by those other feelings.

10

Grief and Family Systems

Although grief is defined as a phenomenon of the emotions, thought, and behavior of a single individual, it is also a phenomenon of relationships among survivors and between bereaved and lost. These are usually family relationships, so an appropriate approach to studying them is from the perspective of family systems theories. This chapter addresses some of the implications of that perspective for grief. Although a thorough family systems analysis centered on the diarists would require data from several members of each family, preferably before and after the loss, important things can be said about grief in a systems perspective with the kind of data the diarists provide.

Resistance to Change

One of the major points in the family systems literature (e.g., Lederer & Jackson, 1968; Wertheim, 1973) that has been well documented is that family systems often resist change. Therapists are interested in understanding and dealing with such resistance because they often find that the effects of individual or family therapy are neutralized by actions and interactions of family members. Families even resist changing through family therapy when they have sought the therapy in order to change. The frequency of resistance to change in therapy situations implies that families also resist change after a loss.

In the grief literature, individual resistance to change has been discussed in terms of initial denial of loss (e.g., Becker, 1973; Donaldson,

1972; Dumont & Foss, 1972; Kubler-Ross, 1969) and in terms of searching for the lost (Bowlby, 1961). That resistance is, in the perspective of the theory of grief work, potentially pathological (see Chapter 3). Theoretical discussions of resistance to change after loss stem from data on the frequency of attempts by bereaved persons early in bereavement to think or act at times as though the loss has not occurred. Both family systems theory and the theory of grief work emphasize the linkage of present resistance to change with past patterns of relationship. The theory of grief work emphasizes the hold on the bereaved of memories and hopes centered on the lost. Family systems theory examines attempts to maintain patterns of relationship as they were before the loss, although whether the mechanism underlying those attempts involves inertia of memories and hopes or some other mechanism is not clearly addressed by various versions of the theory. There are several types of resistance to change in the diary material, expressions of the propensity to maintain things as they were before loss that both the theory of grief work and family systems theory would lead one to expect.

Dreams and a Sense of the Presence of the Lost

The literature on bereavement contains many reports documenting that a substantial number of bereaved people experience a sense of the presence of the person who has died (Clayton, Desmarais, & Winokur, 1968; Glick, Weiss, & Parkes, 1974; Gorer, 1967; Heimlich & Kutscher, 1970; Hobson, 1964; Krupp & Kligfeld, 1962; Lerner, 1981; Marris, 1958, 1974; Matchett, 1972; Parkes, 1970, 1972; Rees, 1971; Wretmark, 1959; Yamamoto, Okonogi, Iwasaki, & Yoshimura, 1969). At times it may be a fleeting impression, and at other times a complex, multisensory, often-repeated impression of substantial duration.

In a previously published cross-cultural analysis of grief and mourning, sense-of-presence phenomena were seen to be linked to the commonality of ghost beliefs cross-culturally (Rosenblatt, Walsh, & Jackson, 1976, chap. 3). Ghost beliefs or ghost experiences are almost universal across cultures, which suggests that ghosts represent common psychic and social dynamics in human life. A close examination of cross-cultural data indicates that the ghosts that people experience are generally of people who were closest to them, implying that these experiences are a product of habitual interaction and of reminders in familiar settings. An analysis of reminders, of the sort that was used in Chapter 9 to understand emotional control and in Chapter 7 to understand differences between leavers in a separation and people who are left, seems to fit the phenomenon of ghost cognitions cross-culturally. People experience ghosts of familiar people because their presence has been strongly associated with familiar stimuli. However, the lost person's continuing absence leads to the familiar stimuli becoming less strongly associated with her or him. The sense of the presence of the lost person tends to occur less frequently, and the "ghost" seems, in the bereaved person's understanding of things, to move to a more distant place or simply to become less interested in and involved with the world of the living.

In the diary data there are several instances of sense of presence. When Katie, her only daughter and only real companion, left on an extended trip, Mary Dodge Woodward reported the following experience.

* * * * * * *

"I have been piecing a comfortable of some old black and red cashmere. It was all spread out on the front room floor when in came Harry [Katie's beau], who I supposed was in Eckleson. I seemed to see Katie on the instant—really to see her—and I was so confused that I hardly knew what to say to him. She has been gone a week—one long week. I get along very well days, but the nights are endless, and I hear every little noise. The gnawing of a mouse kept me awake last night which it does not do when Katie is in bed with me, though it often does her."

Diary of Mary Dodge Woodward (Woodward, 1937, p. 250), entry of October 16, 1888.

* * * * * * *

In this case a person, Katie's beau, provided the stimulus to a sense of presence, and it should be noted that this sense of presence was for someone still alive. A few weeks later, the family's elderly dog, Roxy, died; Woodward wrote the day after the dog's death: "I have had [Roxy] sleep by me since Katie went away. Last night I imagined I heard the patter of her feet; then I would wake and think how tragic it was for the [cow] to toss her to death" (Diary of Mary Dodge Woodward, entry of November 6, 1888, Woodward, 1937, p. 253). In this case the sense of presence seems to have arisen from a dream state. A few days later Woodward seemed to have a sense-of-presence experience for the dog during a waking state: ". . . This is the coldest night we have had this fall. The wind sounds dismal as it whistles around the house; and as the creak of the swinging clothes reel reaches my ears, I fancy I hear poor Roxy cry . . ." (entry of November 10, 1888, Woodward, 1937, p. 255). In this case the stimulus was a sound like that she had heard the dog make.

The first instance of sense of presence in which Woodward thought the dog was still alive arose from a night dream. Dreams provide another instance of the residue of past experience with the lost and another evidence that one cannot automatically forget a relationship and exclude it from one's consciousness simply because it has been ended by a death.

Another diarist whose dreams indicated a disposition to retain a relationship was August Ripley Burbank, who left his wife in the midwest when he started for the California gold fields in 1849. His diary includes the following two dreams of his wife:

* * * * * * *

After 13 days of separation:

"Sabbath. Last night I beheld in the vision of my dream on board of a steam boat on the Illinois River in state room my wife . . . surrounded by her friends whom told me that she had been scalded to death by steam. I was struck with such force on beholding her thus dead that I sank to my knees & when I awoke I was a groaning & deeply weighed down with grief. . . ."

After 120 days of separation:

"In my visionary dream of the night I visited my wife & held sweet converse with her. I awoke much delited that I had again beheld her whome so much had my affections. Soon I fallen asleep and again I beheld her but alas! alas! with what anguish & grievance of Spirit. I was groaning under the weight as I beheld her coffin & a vast concourse of people dressed in mourning & amaking preparation for her burial for the vision said to me that she was dead. I awoke. . . ."

Diary of August Ripley Burbank, unpublished film copy, Bancroft Library, University of California, Berkeley, entries of April 29 and August 14, 1849.

* * * * * * *

In the literature on sense of presence, dreams are not counted as sense-of-presence phenomena. Nonetheless, Burbank's dreams could be interpreted as arising from a disposition to maintain a relationship as it was before loss ("sweet converse"). However, Burbank's dreams also reflect loss and fear of loss. In both his dreams, the wife from whom he was separated appeared as dead. Perhaps he feared that possibility, but perhaps her death in the dreams was a symbolic representation of the separation and the grief he felt over it.

Another diarist who may have experienced a sense of presence was Henry Scadding, a Toronto clergyman whose wife Harriet had died 40 days before the following entry.

* * * * * * *

". . . In administering the [sacramental] cup today, the remembrance of the sweet face of my dear departed Harriet suddenly occurred to me, & quite unmanned me. Oh with what a holy feeling of love did I used there to present to her the sacred emblems of Christ's body & blood! . . ."

Diary of Henry Scadding, unpublished manuscript, Metropolitan Toronto Central Library, entry of November 5, 1843.

* * * * * * *

Scadding's apparent experience of the sense of presence of his wife occurred more than a month after his loss, in contrast to Woodward's sense-of-presence experiences, which came within a few days after her loss. However, Scadding's experience occurred in the face of stimuli with which he had little or no contact since the loss. The sacrament seems to have been the first he had administered since his wife's death. Reminders that set off a sense of presence of a lost person may tend to be clustered early in bereavement and then operate less as reminders as they lose their association with the lost. But sense of presence may occur later in bereavement if one comes in contact with reminders that one has not become used to since the loss occurred. Thus, the sense-of-presence phenomenon is like the resurgence of grief upon first returning to a place important in one's relationship with the lost (Chapter 6). Sense of presence, like sorrow and other aspects of grief, can return repeatedly.

Experiencing the sense of presence of a lost person may be, among other things, a way of saying to oneself that the lost person should be here now. In this setting and this time, Katie should be entering with her beau, Roxy should be nearby, Burbank should be having sweet converse with his wife, or Scadding's wife should be at this sacramental ceremony. It is a way of saying to oneself that it is inappropriate that the lost individual is absent, and in that sense it is a reaching toward a system as it was. It is also a systems phenomenon because other people may stimulate the sense of presence (Katie's beau) and because interaction is often missed (sweet converse, acceptance of the sacramental cup). "Sense of presence" may be an inappropriate label when what is sensed is interaction or interaction about to occur. On those occasions "sense of relationship" might be a more accurate term.

Spiritism

Spiritism, a belief that one could communicate with the spirits of the dead and a method for communicating through seance and spirit medium, became popular in the mid-nineteenth century in North America (Moore, 1975; Nelson, 1969). No diarist from the early part of the century mentioned it, but many diarists writing between 1840 and 1880 did. Some of them, like William H. Brisbane, rejected spiritism.

* * * * * * *

". . . learned some things about the 'Spirit Circle' or 'rappings'. Friend Nicholson is quite a believer in these matters or rather spirits, & Mrs. Flint a widowed sister of Mrs. Hille's is said to be a 'medium'. The family seems very earnest & sincere in their faith in her. I could not myself discover anything mysterious except their evident confidence in these 'manifestations' as they term them. It is very curious how these things originate & progress."

Diary of William H. Brisbane, unpublished manuscript, State Historical Society of Wisconsin, entry of February 3, 1852.

* * * * * * *

There seem to have been multiple sources for the wide acceptance in North American society of spiritism—particularly a moving away from church-controlled religion and an increase in knowledge about electricity, magnetism, and hypnotism (cf. Ahlstrom, 1972, pp. 486-490; Lerner, 1981). The involvement of women as spirit mediums may also be significant, suggesting that one impetus for the growth of spiritism may have been the increasing trend for women to be actively involved in formal religious activities (Welter, 1976, Ch. 6) and in the work force (since some women earned a living as mediums —Moore, 1975). From a family systems perspective, there would be few better ways to maintain a system after the death of one of its members than to believe that one was maintaining contact through spiritist interaction with the person who had died. In fact, Nelson (1969, pp. 267-268) has asserted that the death of a close associate was probably the most common stimulus to membership in the spirit movement. Three of the diarists could be called spiritists; one of them used spiritism in an attempt to communicate with people from whom she was separated.

* * * * * * *

". . . used my best endeavours to mesmerise Mr. Poland, who is a good Clairvoyant, hoping to hear from you. . . ."

Diary of Harriet Sherrill Ward, a 50-year-old woman traveling overland from

Wisconsin to California, leaving children and grandchildren behind. The "you" in this entry were her grown children, for whom she was keeping her diary. Unpublished typescript, Bancroft Library, University of California, Berkeley, entry of September 1, 1853.

* * * * * * *

Ward's attempt to communicate with the children she left behind seems to have been made half seriously, but it makes clear that people believed they could use spiritism in relationships with the living as well as with the dead.

Adeline Brisbane (Addy), the daughter of William Brisbane, who was so skeptical about spiritism, is another diarist who seems to have believed in spiritual communication. Addy's daughter Anna died at the age of two. The day of the child's death her mother wrote: "I thought I should go crazy while she was in those convulsions. . . . Oh, if I could always have her so [in the coffin] even it would be a comfort, she is so beautiful. It seems so hard to put her in the cold ground & hide her lovely face . . ." (Diary of P. Adeline Brisbane, unpublished manuscript, State Historical Society of Wisconsin, entry of September 26, 1868). Two months later the diarist wrote: "We hired a room at Mr. Stickney's for five weeks after [the burial], & then returned here. . . . We have learned not to grieve for our precious angel, yet often the tears will start while singing or thinking of her. Her angel spirit hovers about & often checks me when in the wrong, impatient, etc. I frequently lie awake at night thinking of her . . ." (Diary of P. Adeline Brisbane, entry of December 2, 1868). Apparently the diarist did not attempt communication with her deceased daughter. But she perceived something like spiritual communication coming from the child. Although a single case can be interpreted in many different ways, one possibility is that communication attempts were less likely when the deceased died before developing much capacity to converse. P. Adeline Brisbane had the reassurance of some sort of communication with the daughter she loved so dearly without the frustration of trying to carry on a dialog with the spirit of a toddler.

The diary with most frequent references to spiritist communication is that of Marcus Gunn. As was indicated in Chapter 9, shortly after the death of a grown son, Gunn became deeply enmeshed in what he experienced as spiritual interactions. Here is a set of excerpts from his diary, beginning with the entry reporting the death of his son, James C., and running into the period in which Gunn became actively involved in spiritism.

* * * * * * *

". . . My God . . . my beloved son James Calder Gunn . . . gone from this life. . . . O how desolate we feel now. Our James C. no more to be seen in this life. I returned home under awful depression of mind, under a profound sense of my bereavement. . . . James C.'s age was on the day of his death twenty three years, three months, and three weeks!!!" (entry of December 5, 1853)

". . . Kept retired with Catherine [diarist's second wife, his cousin and the cousin of James C.] in frequent tears thinking of our bereaved condition. Our darling James C. to be seen no more on Earth!!" (entry of December 6, 1853)

". . . I came home . . . absorbed in thoughts about my beloved boys departed, D. Marcus and James C. O, My God will I yet embrace them to part no more. I hope so!! . . . O, the vacancy and bereavement which I now feel. Since yesterday I feel as if my heart was overflowed and arrested in its motion!!" (entry of December 7, 1853)

". . . Letter from my dear brothers Alex and Hugh sealed with black wax — Ominous!! . . . 'With inexpressible grief we have to announce the demise of our most dearly beloved mother. . . .' I need not describe my feelings. . . ." (entry of December 9, 1853)

". . . O, the weighty sense of vacancy, weakness and bereavement which presses upon my mind, when I think of the demise of my boys, D. Marcus and now James C.!!" (entry of December 14, 1853)

". . . O my dear James C. how I feel desolate and empty now without thee!!" (entry of December 16, 1853)

Upon going to pick up his mail — ". . . Alas, Alas! My heart will never be rejoiced as it used to be, on receipt of a letter from my darling Son James C.!!" (entry of December 20, 1853)

"Reading, thinking and reading till 9 P.M. O my darling James C. dost thou still exist? Will I ever embrace thee . . . ?" (entry of December 25, 1853)

". . . My darling Son, James C. O, I hope to embrace him yet & be with him for ever!!" (entry of December 30, 1853)

". . . We feel very desolate at the thoughts of my darling James C. being, for ever, secluded from my eyes, so far as this life is concerned." (entry of December 31, 1853)

". . . Often absorbed in thoughts about my darling boys — D. Marcus & Jas. C. — gone!!" (entry of January 6, 1854)

". . . O my beloved James C. shall I ever meet thee? Ans. yes!!" (entry of January 12, 1854)

". . . Oh Lord God Almighty give me some tangible evidence of the immortality of my beloved ones removed from my sight. I *need* it, oh Lord!!" (entry of January 27, 1854)

". . . I went . . . to a . . . medium of correspondence with departed Spiritists & saw the phenomena of Table Motion & had affected responses with my beloved Boys gone. . . ." (entry of January 29, 1854)

". . . Recd. [newspaper]. It records the demise from this stage of existence of my Sons, D. Marcus and James C. with whom today I had an apparent intercourse – delightful!" (entry of February 4, 1854)

". . . We solicited communications with beloved & departed D. M. & Jas. C. by Mr. Lenee, a writing medium, James C. wrote agreeing with his hand a Memorandum that there was no suitable Medium present." (entry of February 5, 1854)

"[Spiritists] came to visit us. Before and after dinner we had the apparent presence of our beloved D. M. and James C. How happy we felt by their intercourse. How marvelous are the ways O God! . . ." (entry of February 19, 1854)

". . . After tea we sat on the stand. There appeared to be no Medium by which to rise the stand, but on calling on Dona M. three tips were given." (entry of Feburary 23, 1854)

". . . By the medium [Catherine, the diarist's wife] conversed with D. M. & Jas. C. This evening our beloved Jas. C. is three months demised from this life. He and D. M. had converse with C." (entry of February 27, 1854)

". . . Had a delightful and long communication with my beloved sons D. M. and James C. . . ." (entry of March 5, 1854)

". . . After tea we sat at the stand and Catherine's right hand was used by our darling James C. to write!" (entry of March 13, 1854)

". . . Dear Catherine about 10 AM according to promise sat at the stand and as we believe our darling James C. took hold of her hand to practice writing. He wrote his name 'J. C. Gunn.'" (entry of March 14, 1854)

Diary of Marcus Gunn, unpublished typescript, Public Archives of Canada, Ottawa.

* * * * * * *

"Practice," which was mentioned in the entry of March 14 quoted above, was also mentioned in the entries for March 16, 17, 18, and 23. One could argue that the person who was practicing was actually Catherine, the diarist's wife and medium, not the spirit of one of Gunn's deceased sons. From March, 1854, onward, spiritual communication was a frequent and involving part of Marcus Gunn's life, generally with Catherine as medium. Although he communicated with quite a range of "spirits," the communication was richest with the "spirits" of people Catherine knew best and for whom she would have been most accurate in predicting plausible responses. From a systems point of view, the dynamics of the Gunn family are quite interesting. In a sense, Marcus Gunn was retaining the relationship he had with James, his most recently deceased son. But in another sense the relationships in the family were changing, because Catherine became the link between father and son, who had previously communicated directly. Catherine was giving her husband what he most deeply desired, and thus gaining his attention and appreciation. For her that might have been greatly desired at a time when he had been preoccupied with his bereavements and his diary. So at one level, spiritism helped maintain the family interaction pattern as father and son and husband and wife continued to interact, but the pattern was maintained only by the involvement of Catherine (stepmother and wife) in the father-son interactions.

In many ways, Gunn's wife was the perfect medium for him. Not only did she know a great deal about his life after being married to him for several years, but as his cousin she had more information about many aspects of his life before their courtship and marriage than a typical second wife would have had, and more than anybody else living in Gunn's home or community. Because of her knowledge, she could overcome any skepticism about spiritist communication Gunn may have had. For example, on March 19, 1854, Gunn wrote "we had converse with . . . my Father [who had died in 1832] who answered 17 questions correctly. . . ." This interest in getting correct answers to questions seems to indicate skepticism, either about spiritism in general or about the professed identity of the specific "spirit." Over the years, the circle of deceased people with whom Gunn communicated expanded. He eventually communicated with the spirits of additional relatives who had died before March, 1854, with those who died after that date, and with the "spirit" associates of the deceased he had known in life and of the occasional mediums recruited in place of Catherine.

As time passed since a death, Gunn's spiritist communications with a dead person became less frequent. Presumably many factors were involved—other losses intervened and were more salient; there were fewer reminders of the lost; life had come to be whole without need for communication with the lost; and the standard repertory of things a spirit was understood to be able to communicate made for increasingly redundant communication. But the way Gunn and his circle seem to have understood this decline in communication was that it was a matter of choice by the spirit. The spirit became increasingly involved with affairs of the spirit world and chose to keep its distance from the living. For example, Gunn wrote in 1874 of his daughter Joanna, who died in 1871 at age 49, "On my inquiring of [a spirit] why my darling Spirit daughter Joanna does not, now, find facility for communicating with me? The reply was that she was, now, attracted to the family above, with attractions to Earth abated . . ." (entry of July 7, 1874).

In the cross-cultural study of ghost beliefs, spirits of the deceased generally are perceived by people with ghost beliefs as moving farther away over time (Rosenblatt, Walsh, & Jackson, pp. 63-65). Such perception of movement can be expected if people have effectively carried out part or all of their grief work or engaged in some sort of self-conscious cutting of ties with the deceased in order to function. In either case the significance of potential reminders of the lost can be expected to change, either because people come in contact with the reminders recurrently without the lost person being present or because they have actively worked at changing the meanings of the reminders. The same sort of process seems to have operated in the case of Marcus Gunn; the spirits he cared about tended to move farther away. The distance was experienced, in part, as a movement away by the spirits, who were perceived as becoming less interested in earthly matters (cf. Ahern's 1973 analysis of contact with the spirits of deceased kin in a Chinese community in northern Taiwan). Although spiritist communication may be an attempt to maintain a family system as it has been, it seems more often to delay change or to spread the pain of change over a longer period.

Prayer

Another way in which people seem to work at preserving a family system is by prayers for those lost through separation or death. Without in any way questioning the spiritual meanings of prayer, one can also look at it from social-science and psychological perspectives. From a family system perspective, it seems plausible that by saying prayers for someone now dead, a person could be maintaining the same concerned and caring relationship that was present before the loss occurred. However, in another sense the person may be shifting some responsibility onto the deity to whom the prayer is directed. Thus, with prayer a person may be retaining one aspect of a relationship, while acknowledging that another is being relinquished. Prayer may say "I care about you," but also "somebody else or something else has to watch over you." Thus, prayer may be a way of both holding on to a relationship and acknowledging its change.

Prayer *to* the lost may be a way of maintaining a relationship, if it was one in which the lost person was somehow beneficent. But even then the prayer may express a sense of relationship change. Exactly one year after his mother was buried, Archibald Gillies entered the following prayer in his diary.

* * * * * * *

". . . Watch o'er us, kindly, mother dear. Keep us in the right way so when our time does come to go we will not wish to stay (here)."

Diary of Archibald L. Gillies, unpublished manuscript, Ontario Archives, entry of April 12, 1894.

* * * * * * *

His prayer seems to have continued a recognition of his mother's nurturance and power, but it also seems to acknowledge change, to be saying that he counts on her for support now only in the spiritual area. In fact, prayer for material help would have been quite risky. Were the "help" not given, the diarist would have to face the apparent lack of nurturance of the lost person's "spirit."

Reunion in Heaven

* * * * * * *

"'No more shall the bosom, when heaving with anguish,
In the kind breast of sympathy seek for relief;
While helpless I wander; or hopeless I languish,
Ah! cold is the heart that would share all my grief.'
Consuming thought! Who shall ever wipe the tear of sorrow from these weeping eyes, or lend the ear of undissembled sympathy to the complaints of my broken heart. Who shall bend with the smile of tenderness over the bed of suffering [the diarist was about eight months pregnant], and cheer me with the voice of affection. Alas! Alas! *no* change can ever restore *him* to these widowed arms; and I should go down to the grave in sorrow, were it not that God is my helper. This sweet hope of meeting in heaven, it cheers and animates, and renders life supportable."

Diary of Susan Mansfield Huntington, unpublished manuscript, Sterling Memorial Library, Yale University, entry of November 9, 1819, about two months after her husband died.

* * * * * * *

Many diarists, in a first entry reporting a loss or in the early entries after it, wrote that "we will meet in heaven." From a family systems point of view, perhaps nothing could be more effective in maintaining the system than a continuing aspiration to resume contact. For Susan Mansfield Huntington, the list of things her husband had formerly done for her and that she so sorely missed was followed by a statement that life was rendered supportable by the thought of reuniting with him in heaven. From a systems viewpoint she was not working at changing the system (though obviously it was changing) but was counting on a reunion, or thoughts of one, to make tolerable her continued hold on a remnant of the system.

People work at maintaining a family system. However, the idea of reuniting in heaven seems not to have much earthly reality for the diarists who wrote about such reunions. "Reunion in heaven" seemed to be remote from worldly concerns; diarists did not expect to tell things to the deceased or ask questions of them, or to get help with problems they had been trying to solve. No diarist wrote "I must remember to ask X that when we meet in heaven." Thus, expecting or hoping for reunion in heaven, like the sense of presence of the lost, spiritual communication, and prayer, seems unable to retain a system as it was. Although people were in some sense attempting to prevent change and may have succeeded in postponing it, the reality of a life without the lost person required that change eventually occur.

Using the Wishes of the Lost as a Guide to Action

Some diarists claimed that they were doing something because it was what a dead relative would want them to do. This is not uncommon among contemporary bereaved persons (Bowlby & Parkes, 1970). To some extent it may be a way of honoring the dead person. From a systems viewpoint, acting on the wishes of the dead could be a way of maintaining a system. To the extent that the other person had a policy-making role in the system, acting on the policies that person established or would have been expected to establish may help maintain the system. However, to the extent that one acts more on the lost person's wishes now than in the past, the system actually has changed. And the absence of fresh legislation from the person now lost makes it unclear, no matter what the past system was, whether or not one is acting on one's own fantasy. That may be why most of the action by the diarists on wishes of the dead involved only distribution of the property of the lost and disposal of the body.

Substitutions for the Lost

Finding Someone Else to Do the Work of a Spouse

Once the reality of a loss is accepted, perhaps the next line of defense in maintaining a system is to substitute somebody for the lost person. Bowlby and Parkes (1970) have argued that role problems are, after emotional problems, the most immediate concern in bereavement. Role substitution is generally difficult to deduce from the diaries. No diarist wrote of subtle role differences in relationships. The more concrete role differences—who cooked meals or watched children—were reported by some diarists, but often in passages that are difficult to interpret. Many people could do the work associated with the opposite sex; for example, male Forty-Niners seemed to have no trouble cooking and doing laundry, and some women found that they could do farm work if they had to. But people in the nineteenth century seemed to have a strong sense of propriety about gender-related work. Women were supposed to do women's work and men were supposed to do men's work. Perhaps that is why the seeking of a substitute if the only adult of the opposite sex in the household were lost seemed common in the lives of bereaved diarists. A diarist might change residence—to move in with someone who could do opposite-sex work—or go away from home for a service (such as laundry or cooking) previously obtained at home. However, those changes were often reported in a way that allowed for a variety of interpretations. Consider, for example, the entry which E. B. Drew made in his diary a week after his wife left Minnesota for the east.

* * * * * * *

"I got tired of going it alone. Go to Stewarts for my meals."

Diary of Edward Bolivar Drew, unpublished manuscript, Minnesota Historical Society, entry of October 25, 1859.

* * * * * * *

This entry is typical of those reporting changes after a loss. Role substitution seems to have occurred, but it may have been tangential to more important matters. Was Drew eating with the Stewarts because of his incompetence at cooking or because he lacked the time to cook well? Or was he still cooking for himself but doing it at the Stewarts' house? Was he lonely? The diary does not disclose his motivation, and the question of what sort of role substitution was occurring remains difficult to answer.

Some diarists may have taken in a housekeeper or hired hand after the loss of somebody who was the sole source of work typically done by the opposite sex. But it is difficult to keep track of the comings and goings of hired help, because many diarists seem to have considered them inappropriate to enter in a diary. Thus, a maid might be mentioned at one entry in a long series, without any clue to when she arrived or left. Or a diarist might have mentioned the return of a hired hand whose leaving (and even, perhaps, whose previous presence) had not been recorded.

The loss that most often led to concern about substitution seemed to be the loss of a spouse. People did not write about getting a new sibling, new child, or new parent, although minors who had lost a parent were sometimes moved to a relative's house. The need for a spouse encompasses an enormous number of needs, wants, habits, concerns, and customs (cf. Gage, 1975). Perhaps the most prominent needs of diarists after the loss of a spouse were the following:

1. Need for the labor of the opposite sex.

2. Need for a legal representative. Women in many parts of North America in the nineteenth century had fewer legal rights than men and might not have any right to their house, farm, or personal property, including property that they themselves brought into the marriage (Scott, 1962).

3. Need for a protector. Women of the more respectable classes seemed to need a male protector or guardian in order to remain respectable, particularly in the frontier areas and at times of civil unrest.

4. Need of a caretaker for children. A mother's milk was an obvious need for a baby, and there were no day care institutions for a young child whose single parent was deeply involved in work. A single father seemed to need either a surrogate parent for younger children or a place to board them.

5. Sexual needs. Sex was never spoken of as a need by any widowed diarist, but it seems unlikely that the people of the nineteenth century had no sexual needs.

6. Affection and companionship, including touching, conversation, and adult human presence. Perhaps many expressions of grief for a spouse reflected these needs, although few diarists spoke about them in precisely those terms.

Male and female diarists who lost spouses seemed to differ in the way they sought substitutes, and in the substitute typically chosen. The five widowers with young children either had a female present (a maid, sister, or granddaughter) almost immediately after the loss of a spouse or soon placed the children elsewhere. Widows in the sample never boarded a young child out, although two sent older, perhaps difficult-to-manage sons to boarding school. Five of the seven widows in the sample either had adults (including slaves) living with them at the onset of widowhood or quickly moved in with other adults. Widows seemed to live with other adults as a result of other factors than the need for help in child care, except in the case of Susan Mansfield Huntington, who had six children and was pregnant at the time of her husband's death.

Laws in the early part of the nineteenth century left most married women without control of income and assets, even assets a woman brought into the marriage and income earned by her (Basch, 1979). Consequently, a widow might well find herself without control of the assets from her marriage, and might even be evicted from her own dwelling. Beyond property considerations, norms of respectability in the early part of the nineteenth century seemed to demand that a woman not live without "protectors." Later in the century, laws dealing with marital property changed somewhat, and living without another adult apparently became more acceptable. The two widows who seemed to be living without an adult companion were widowed in the 1860s.

God as Substitute

Susan Mansfield Huntington, whose belief that she would meet her deceased husband in heaven was discussed earlier in this chapter, often spoke of God as serving somehow as her husband.

* * * * * * *

"Six months have elapsed since my affliction & it is as fresh as it was at first. Will it always be so? But the very *thought* of remembering him less seems like unfaithfulness to one whom I had the best reasons for loving. God has been inexpressibly good to me. In his mercy he gave me the boy, dear image of his father, to bear his name, & in some measure fill the awful chasm [which] the long, long absence of that father has made in my family & my heart. . . . I surmise that this stroke may even drive me to God as my husband & my portion. . . ."

Diary of Susan Mansfield Huntington, unpublished manuscript, Sterling Memorial Library, Yale University, entry of March 6, 1820.

* * * * * * *

The notion of God as husband is not so bizarre if one realizes that her husband had been a minister and that she was living in an era in which husbands were often patriarchal. Moreover, the Bible may be read as encouraging one to make that type of substitution. For example, the King James Version of the Bible offers this translation of a passage in Isaiah: "[Thou] . . . shalt not remember the reproach of thy widowhood any more. For thy Maker is thine husband . . ." (Isaiah 54:4-5). But of course one cannot imagine God serving a full range of husband functions, and that might well be true for any role substitution—it is imperfect because the substitute does not provide exactly what was missed, so the family system tends to change. God is an interesting choice of substitute for a husband in that He provides emotional support, strength, wisdom, and other patriarchal services while being nonsexual. If it can be assumed that widows were considered wicked if sexually involved soon after the loss of a husband, and if many widows did not want a sexual relationship soon after the loss, a male role substitute for a lost husband would have had to be one with well-controlled or no lust. A twentieth-century study of Boston widows found many widows turning to a brother of the husband as a substitute (Parkes & Bowlby, 1970). Presumably a husband's brother would be able to sustain a past pattern of benevolent, nonsexual interaction. The Boston study also reported that the relationship did not persist, perhaps in part because the widow's needs changed but perhaps also because the substitution was inadequate. Susan Mansfield Huntington seems to have lacked a brother-in-law or any other male who could substitute for her husband. So for her turning to God may have been the only option.

The only other loss for which God was ever mentioned as a possible substitute was the loss of a parent. No diarist spoke of God as a possible substitute for a lost wife or child. Children may sometimes have been encouraged by a widowed mother to substitute God for a lost father. Susan Mansfield Huntington, who is quoted above as seeing God as a substitute for her husband, wrote this of one of her children.

* * * * * * *

"My youngest child (her father's darling *because* the youngest) is quite unwell. I feel as if I loved her better than ever because she appears to feel her loss in her father so much. She evidently misses him, & is lonesome. . . . The dear little creature said this morning of her own accord 'Ma I have no father but God. I *will* ask God to be my father. I *will* love God, & go to heaven & see Papa.' She often says this, and when I say 'I love you dearly', she replies, 'And pa loves me too.' She seems unwilling to lose the recognition of this relation. Precious precious children, precious father. God grant we may make *one* happy family in heaven."

Diary of Susan Mansfield Huntington, unpublished manuscript, Sterling Memorial Library, Yale University, entry of November 23, 1819.

* * * * * * *

The child saw God as a substitute father, but she also hung on to the possibility of reunion in Heaven and, unlike adults, seems to have seen some reality in the notion that she could reunite with her father in heaven.

Remarriage

If diarists found surrogate parents, turning, for example, to a more mature neighbor for emotional support, they left no mention of it. The clearest traces of role substitutes in the diaries were the instances of remarriage. No elderly diarist whose spouse had died seems to have remarried; several lived out their days in the homes of grown children. But four widowed diarists under age 60—Burge, Drew, Cheever, and Phillips—did remarry during the period covered by the diary volumes examined. (Grigg, 1977, summarizing age effects in her data and in other historical studies of remarriage, reports strong trends toward more frequent remarriage at younger age of spouse loss.) The courtship of these diarists typically left little trace in their diaries, but it seems clear that for some of them remarriage was a matter of convenience, that they were ambivalent about remarrying or about the new spouse. For example, Dolly Lunt Burge, who was widowed three times, wrote the following two passages at the time of deciding to marry her second and third husbands.

* * * * * * *

". . . What have I done? Am I not dreaming? What means it all? Why these heavy forebodings. . . . I have often joked & laughed about marrying & though I have when asked always refused yet I am caught this time. Is my heart truly interested? Do I love him to whom I am about to commit my all of earthly happiness? Can I take upon myself the most solemn of all oaths to Love, Honour & Obey one to whom I am so utterly a stranger? How can I tell but that my feelings & affections may prove recreant to my judgment and that I may be sowing to myself thorns and briars that may afterwards sorely sting and annoy me . . ." (December 29, 1849).

". . . After meeting was over Dr. Thomas handed me a letter which I put in my pocket carelessly. . . . What was my surprise when at Mrs. Graves' I took it out & found it to be from 'Uncle Billy' stating his intention of visiting me on the ensuing Tuesday in view of a matrimonial connection. O how I wished he had never written it . . ." (July 22, 1866).

Diary of Dolly Lunt Burge (1962, pp. 31, 121-122).

* * * * * * *

Her ambivalence about the two men whom she subsequently married may have stemmed from many sources. Women seemed under substantial pressure to be married, particularly younger women. Few occupations open to them provided adequate subsistence, and farming, even with the help of slaves (Burge lived in Georgia) or male hired hands, was difficult for them.

Ambivalence seems to be more prominent and love less prominent in diary entries describing plans to remarry then in entries describing plans for a first marriage. The subsequent marriages of the diarists seem to have been dictated primarily by economic and role necessity, although love was encouraged to develop. In the one case in which economic and role needs were not salient, Martin W. Phillips may have anticipated that a planned second marriage might be punishing because his first marriage was.

Substitution and the Parent-Child Relationship

The passage from the Huntington diary dealing with her youngest daughter's grief touches on another systems phenomenon, the interaction of griefs. When a family member dies, everybody grieves, and interactions and interaction problems hinge to some extent on the degree to which each person is a stimulus for the grief of the others (Silverman & Silverman, 1979), and on how the different griefs blend. If one can believe Huntington's diary, the child's expression of grief was in a sense supportive of the mother's. The child said things that agreed with the mother's perspective and sense of loss and, in this case, even agreed with her notion of a substitute for the lost father. A number of other diarists cited statements by their children that seemed to support their own point of view. Surely an element of this was the child's response to parental expression of needs, wants, and approval. At the extreme, some children were seen by a diarist as expressing grief over a person who died before the child was born. Perhaps the child felt something like grief, but those feelings might well have been implanted in the child.

In some contemporary families, problems arise in bereavement because there is no consensus about who will substitute for the person who has died (Jensen & Wallace, 1967). Family members disagree about who should take on what functions, a function is thrust on a person who is unwilling or unable to assume it, or some necessary function is not assumed.

The single-parent situation seems to have been a source of such problems in nineteenth-century families. Apparently it was rare, in the nineteenth century, for a man with preteen children to attempt to raise them himself; the diary examples of problems in single parenting with young children are all in entries written by mothers. A widow might, for example, have trouble doing some chore herself or trying to get a child to do it. That does not mean that the children were necessarily uncooperative. In some cases they were more than willing to help, but were simply unable. Young children who had lost a father might often express a strong but unrealistic intent to help.

* * * * * * *

". . . I wish I could have dagguerotyped [Johnny's] countenance and attitude as he said yesterday 'Mamma, I'm not afraid. I'll stay by *you*. If Indian come, I'll chop his head right off'. . . ."

Diary of Mrs. William B. Dodd, unpublished manuscript, Minnesota Historical Society, entry of September 11, 1862. Mr. Dodd had been killed two weeks before in a battle with Sioux Indians.

* * * * * * *

Johnny was, of course, not in a position to do what he thought he should, and was mistaken in what he seems to have considered his mother's prime need. In another entry Mrs. Dodd complained about the children not doing a competent job in the cornfield, and of an older boy's reluctance to help. His reluctance may have stemmed in part from his inability to do what was asked, although simple obstreperousness may also have been involved.

Mothers and children also seem often to have disagreed about decorum for children, especially bereaved children. An example can be found in the rich diary of Susan Mansfield Huntington.

* * * * * * *

"I now give myself up wholly to my Saviour; & I give all mine wholly to Him. Oh for my children! Two of them have been uncommonly obstinate & boisterous of late, owing in part perhaps to my having been unable to pay as much attention to them as I ought. Yesterday before meeting in correcting one of them I found myself too much excited, & was more angry than I could be without '*sin*.' It interrupted greatly my enjoyment. . . ."

Diary of Susan Mansfield Huntington, unpublished manuscript, Sterling Memorial Library, Yale University, entry of March 19, 1821.

* * * * * * *

For a thirty-year-old widow with seven children, Huntington was probably doing well to function at all. She may have set unrealistically high standards for herself and her children, and she may have, in the past, counted on her husband's help in managing the children.

It was not uncommon in the diaries in the sample, and in other diaries not included because there was no instance of loss, for fathers to beat children (cf. Sunley, 1955). Even children under a year old might be beaten for some transgression. Some women diary keepers expressed disapproval of such whipping, although they seemed unable or unwilling to stop it, and engaged in the practice themselves. The following example from the diary of Mary Richardson Walker is unusual in the involvement of the mother in physical punishment but otherwise not atypical of instances of severe punishment in the diaries.

* * * * * * *

"About ten o'clock in the morning Elkanah [a two-year-old boy] asked for some sugar. I told him to say 'please sugar,' but he refused but continued to cry, 'I want some sugar.' I thought best to try the rod which I continued to do with increasing severity till his father came when I delivered him to him, and he followed the same course till noon when the child became so much exhausted that we concluded to let him sleep but he did not seem to yield at all. . . . We thought not to allow food or drink tell [sic] he should say please some, but if he asked for milk & we told him to say 'please milk,' he would say 'I dont [sic] want to say please'. . . . In the morning, Apr. 1st, we again tried to compel him to yield but he was still firm. We used the rod till we feared to longer. We tried to tempt him with food & drink but to no effect altho he had taken not a drop of any thing for more than 24 hours. . . ." (entry dated March 31, 1846, although it refers to April 1)

". . . We concluded to release our poor little boy. After he was dressed he wanted, he said, to go out & see the bright sun. At breakfast he several times said please when he wanted any thing without being told. I regret the course we pursued tho I do not perceive that he is injured by it except for the time but less severity would I think have been just as well. I often fear being guilty of the very thing for which I punish my child. . . ." (entry of April 2, 1846)

Diary of Mary Richardson Walker (1963, pp. 294-295).

* * * * * * *

Children growing up in such a family might become quite difficult when the bearer of the rod left or died. They may not have internalized values as children might in a less punitive system of control. The same problem may be present for a surviving spouse—the loss of husband or wife removes the forces that kept the surviving spouse doing chores or other activities. Consider, for example, the following excerpt.

* * * * * * *

"To my great grief a spirit of indolence steals over me today. . . . let me waste no time in talking, in sleeping but steadily work. Oh I fear to fall into careless, easy ways. I have now my freedom, no check no."

Diary of Mrs. William B. Dodd, unpublished manuscript, Minnesota Historical Society, entry of September 14, 1862, about 19 days after the death of her husband, who seems to have been a general in the militia.

* * * * * * *

Child-Naming and the Seeking of a Substitute

The social and psychological processes that underlie the naming of a child after someone else are undoubtedly complex. Naming a child after someone who has died might be seen as an attempt to find a psychological or emotional substitute for the lost person. Yet, as the following quote from the diary of the mother of a new baby suggests, the substitution was imperfect for some people, who found it difficult to use the old name in a new way.

* * * * * * *

". . . We call him George, George Rice. This is dear Charlie's wish as well as mine. I am so glad it can be so. . . . I can not call him George yet; it seems too sacred a name to speak aloud. O my poor dear brother, if I might only see you once again on earth, but I may meet you in Heaven."

Diary of Mrs. Charles C. Carpenter, unpublished filmed copy, Public Archives of Canada, Ottawa, entry of November 13, 1863. The first George Rice was the diarist's brother, whose death she had learned of in June.

* * * * * * *

If inhibitions about using the name can be overcome—if, for example, the Carpenters had begun to call their new son "George"—the name substitution may reduce the potency of the name as a stimulus to grief by changing its meaning.

Disputes over Succession to Ownership

Another form in which grief might interact within a family system is through dispute over inheritance. Such disputes can seriously disrupt relationships, particularly among siblings (Titus, Rosenblatt, &

Anderson, 1979). Disputes may arise over disagreements about what is a fair or equal division of property, or over the wishes of the deceased. For example, several months after her father died, P. Adeline Brisbane wrote the following.

* * * * * * *

". . . That night Brother, Em, & I sat up until about 1 o'clock. . . . talking over affairs about Mother. . . . Brother thinks as Father left him sole executor and as he previously had given up to him the care of all the property that he intended him to attend to the crops & every thing for Mother giving her all the income (after expenses were paid) for her support, and I too am confident of it. But Will and Mother think she has a right to every thing (except perhaps the actual real estate) to take at any time and give it all away (crops & all) if she wishes, without paying any taxes on the property or Brother having anything to do or say about it. Oh we had a dreadful time about it yesterday because Brother told Will he had the management of Mother's affairs and wished it would not interfere with his business so much. If any one says a word or even hints against anything Will says or does Mother dislikes the person speaking more & likes Will better. Will always was officious naturally and now talks as if no one would or could attend to Mother & her affairs as well as himself."

Diary of P. Adeline Brisbane, unpublished manuscript, State Historical Society of Wisconsin, entry of August 21, 1878.

* * * * * * *

From the point of view of family systems, family inheritance disputes may arise in part because bereaved people may be less flexible. Their emotions may make them unwilling or unable to behave alternatively or to compromise. Moreover, the normal anger of bereavement may find a target in an apparently covetous sibling or offspring. If the person who died was a family peacemaker, as the elder Brisbane seems to have been, the death may also remove the peace mechanism the disputants usually relied on. The object of a dispute may be real estate with subsistence value, as was the case in the Brisbane family, or may be chattels of sentimental value, as seems to have been the case in the following example.

* * * * * * *

". . . I received a box of some of mother's things, a shawl and dress that I gave her, Grandmother Baker's shears & spectacles that mother kept for years, and her pitcher too, a blue one, a buff dress, a quilt, a night sack & chemise, 16 night-caps, several (4) collars & cuffs (3); a pair of crochet cuffs and mother's earrings (that she had worn 48 years), & some piecework to Sarah [diarist's daughter], besides several little trinkets (shells, beads, fan, etc.), a pair of knit cuffs, the last knitting mother ever done, & a chair cover that mother made. I will keep those little relics that mother kept, in remembrance of her I loved. She is gone. I can see her here no more. It seems too bad that she worked & worked so many years and the things she intended for us (her girls) are to be kept by Agnes & Henry [sister-in-law and brother of the diarist]. Tis all we can do. I am sure they will not enjoy them."

Diary of Emily Hawley Gillespie, unpublished transcript, State Historical Society of Iowa, Iowa City, entry of October 13, 1882. As tensions subsequently developed, it became clear that Gillespie's most intense claims were to $200, which was certainly of more than sentimental value, and to a chest of drawers.

* * * * * * *

Shoulders to Cry on and People to Help

In the area of support it is also appropriate to look at grief in terms of relationship systems rather than as an individual phenomenon. It is commonly understood in North American culture now, and seems to have been in the nineteenth century, that having a shoulder to cry on helps assuage grief. The evolutionary significance of grief may lie in part in motivating others to provide assistance and in motivating the bereaved to maintain contact with others (Averill, 1968). In fact, lack of support may augment feelings of bereavement. For example, the absence of somebody to provide tenderness and support seems to be part of what saddened Susan Mansfield Huntington when she wrote the following diary entry.

* * * * * * *

"To-morrow is the Annual Thanksgiving. These are sad days to me. They seem like landmarks of the soul, whose periodical recurrence, present at one glance, all the varieties of each . . . stage of the way. I have been called to number one, & another, & another; since he who once travelled with me has been called home. My *children* too! my sweet Joshua. Yes! I am written 'widow & disolute.' [sic] Others have a parent, a brother, a sister, to mingle with them the aspirations of gratitude, or the tears of sympathy: but to me, there is not a dear relative who bears these endearing names, on whose bosom I can repose, & feel the sweet glow of confiding tenderness. No! these ties are all swept away. And I *must* feel it. An heart like mine could not have been called to surrender one after another of what it so dearly loved & not entertain at seasons like *this* some keen sense of its desolation. Yet hush every dissatisfied thought, oh my soul! Thy greatest mercies have been sweetly mingled with thy heaviest trials, & God has proved himself good & kind in all."

Diary of Susan Mansfield Huntington, unpublished manuscript, Sterling Memorial Library, Yale University, entry of December 4, 1822.

* * * * * * *

Huntington was not always without support, and she seemed to appreciate the support given by her children. Several weeks after her husband's death she wrote, "I have great comfort in my children who appear to feel anxious to promote my happiness . . ." (unpublished manuscript, Sterling Memorial Library, Yale University, entry of October 12, 1819). Having people act as though they care may be supportive (and having people act as though they do not care may be very painful), but support may not always be a blessing. When Sophia Sewell Wood returned to her childhood home ten weeks after the death of her husband, the sympathy that she received there seems to have been counterbalanced by the pain of comparing her condition with that of women who had not lost a husband.

* * * * * * *

"I am rejoiced to see [my female relatives]. . . . & yet I feel my own disconsolate situation in all its force. They have husbands that they love, & in the bosom of their sweet families taste that real content & enjoyment that are sought in vain through the giddy world."

Diary of Sophia Sewell Wood, unpublished manuscript, Sterling Memorial Library, Yale University, entry of May 19, 1810.

* * * * * * *

The sympathy of others, although Wood appreciated it at times, became burdensome. The sameness of it, the obligation to be politely receptive to it and to appear to have feelings of deserving of sympathy might all have been affecting her when she wrote the following.

* * * * * * *

"E'en the pittying [sic] tear of many friends & soft compassion becomes irksome & tedious to a heart oppressed." (entry of July 12, 1810)

* * * * * * *

Sometimes people tried to help her by telling her how much worse off they had been. Sympathy in the form of I've-been-there-before-and-felt-worse can generally be expected to be a burden to a bereaved person, and Wood seems to have experienced it that way.

* * * * * * *

"I received a gentle reprimand from my good uncle for indulging my feelings & nourishing woe. He in vain endeavoured to convince me he had been far more afflicted than myself & began to narrate a tale of sufferings that were indeed severe . . . tho long gone bye, the mention of produced the very grief he try'd to stifle in me. I too could sympathize & not alone with him, for my beloved Father was one of the numerous family he mourned. . . . The recital of so many sad events far from lessening, increased each painful emotion & ere twas half finished, my uncle required himself the consolation he in vain essayed to give me. . . ." (entry of July 14, 1810)

* * * * * * *

Wood's reactions suggest that social support in grief may be a burden at times rather than a help. Yet the burdening may actually be helpful in dealing with the grief. If the support is in some ways a trial, the bereaved person may reduce grieving in order to escape the unpleasant support. If support is rewarding, one may be in some ways disposed to continue grieving. So support that is at least partly a burden may help one move beyond the point of most intense grief.

The expression of another's grief, as in the entry in which Sophia Wood described her uncle's attempt to help, may push one to be supportive of others, and this may be helpful to a bereaved person in several ways. In fact, a number of bereaved diarists seemed to say that. But helping others does not seem to have been motivated by a desire to help oneself, but rather to have arisen out of ordinary empathy processes. In their bereavement many diarists thought of others who would also be upset because of the loss. The following passage, quoted in part at the beginning of Chapter 6, illustrates the almost reflexive concern that commonly occurred at the initial report of an upsetting loss.

* * * * * * *

"Got letter . . . *Mamas Death Oh!* how bad, shocking. . . . Poor Charles. How I pity him. God help him he has yet to hear the news. God help my sister and Father, and me. We all need it."

Diary of Alfred F. Armstrong, unpublished manuscript, Archives of Ontario, entry of September 25, 1863.

* * * * * * *

Several men who had lost a wife seemed extremely depressed at first, but their concern about their children seems to have pushed them out of the depths.

* * * * * * *

". . . Were it not that I seem to be needed here, how gladly would I lie down in death and be at rest from all these sorrows that gnaw at my soul like a carnivorous animal. . . ."

Diary of Dustin G. Cheever, unpublished manuscript, State Historical Society of Wisconsin, Whitewater Regional Historical Center, entry of Feburary 8, 1873, about a month after the death of his wife.

* * * * * * *

Cheever's depression can be interpreted from a family systems viewpoint as in part an expression of a desire to reunite with his deceased wife. It seems clear also that the needs of his children, perhaps particularly of a son with a severely injured arm, motivated him to work at controlling his grief and in some ways to withdraw from his loss, or at least from his depression over it.

Support of others may require from a bereaved person the supression or concealment of some of the grief, putting on a front less bereaved than one's internal feelings. Consider, for example, the following excerpt from the diary of Sophia Wood.

* * * * * * *

". . . am extremely anxious . . . to once more return to my poor distressed father [in-law] who mourns the loss of his darling Son. I'll go to him . . . to mitigate his woes & smile to cheer him while my own heart is bursting. . . ."

Diary of Sophia Sewell Wood, unpublished manuscript, Sterling Memorial Library, Yale University, entry of May 1, 1810.

* * * * * * *

Although one may feel very intensely the discrepancy between one's external expression of cheer or equanimity and one's internal feelings of grief, working at putting on a cheerful front may actually reduce the feelings of grief. Thus, although Wood may have felt the grief, while she was putting on a more positive front for her father-in-law she may have felt less bereaved, and this effect may have lingered after she had left her father-in-law.

Helping others may also distract one from one's grief. Focusing on another may remove one's attention from one's own feelings about a loss or change perspective on the loss. Susan Mansfield Huntington wrote about distraction in the following terms.

* * * * * * *

". . . When I am pouring the prayers of my soul for others . . . my own sorrow is lessened also. I feel that I am but *one* member of the general body, that by diffusing my sympathies & my sorrows to *all* the members their intenseness is softened, their effects chastised & elevated, & what *would* have led me to . . . despair, felt for myself *alone*, diffused only diverts my mind from itself & drives me, I hope, to a throne of grace. . . ."

Diary of Susan Mansfield Huntington, unpublished manuscript, Sterling Memorial Library, Yale University, entry of June 22, 1820.

* * * * * * *

The act of helping another may also draw one closer to the other. Nurturing and being nurtured, helping and being helped, are part of what builds close, warm, and sometimes intense relationships. Particularly when two people have a gap in their lives created by a loss, which leaves them with needs unmet and with the time that used to be spent with the deceased available to spend with others, a mutual helping process may draw these two people closer. People in the present day often say that a death drew them closer to somebody, and some diarists also found a death drawing them closer to somebody. Elisha Lord Cleaveland, a New Haven minister whose brother died in December, 1863, wrote the following in his diary.

* * * * * * *

". . . This has been a most precious visit from this dear sister. The death of dear brother John has drawn her closer to me than ever. . . ."

Diary of Elisha Lord Cleaveland, Sterling Memorial Library, Yale University, entry of April 26, 1864.

* * * * * * *

It is not clear in the Cleaveland diary what drew sister and brother together, but in the following passage from the diary of Lester Ward, some of the processes that may be operating seem evident.

* * * * * * *

"Little did I dream three weeks ago that I should have to recount today the loss of my precious baby, my sweet son! . . . He was buried at Rome beside his mother's grandmother. . . . We spent several days visiting there with our friends, and came back. Since our return I have borrowed fifty dollars from Joe Young, and we are trying to cheer up. We go everywhere, and do not stay at home much in the evening. . . . I think that our mutual love has increased since the death of our sweet son. I adore my blessed wife, the joy and idol of my heart."

Diary of Lester Ward, entry of June 3, 1866 (Ward, 1935, pp. 201-202).

* * * * * * *

In trying to cheer themselves and each other, the Wards may have been interacting more than before the loss, working at being supportive, and going to entertaining places. This is not to say that sharing a common disaster lacks its own elements for drawing people together. The shared horror that sets the bereaved apart from others, empathic feelings, the realization that one could lose the other and be in an even worse position, may all help to draw people bereaved for the same loss together. But working at supporting each other provides additional processes that may help draw them together.

Summary and Conclusions

This chapter has examined grief from the perspective of the roles and sentiments in family systems. The diaries contain many illustrations of the resistance of family systems to change after a loss —dreams and the sense of presence of the lost person, the attempt to communicate with the lost by means of a spirit medium, the attempt to retain a relationship with the lost through prayer to the lost or to God, the hope of being reunited with the lost, and the use of the wishes of the lost as a guide to action. There are, however, indications that these attempts to retain a system as it was actually subverted it. Dreams of the lost and the sense of his or her presence tell one that the lost is actually gone. Spiritist communications apparently cannot be sustained, and even the process of communicating through a medium alters the relationship. Prayer to the lost tends to deal only with the spiritual area, in which the risk of being rejected by the lost person is relatively slight. And prayer to God, even if expressing a continued concern for the lost, is an acknowledgment that one cannot help the lost. Planning to reunite in heaven with a deceased person also seems to reflect the awareness of change, since the plans reported in the diaries never included mundane content. Finally, following the wishes of the lost seems to reflect awareness of change, in that reference to wishes seem rare after the first weeks of bereavement.

Another family systems phenomenon reflected in the diaries was seeking substitutes for the lost, trying to maintain the system as it was while changing the occupant of the role. Men more than women seemed to turn to others for help with young children; women turned more than men to God as a substitute spouse. But many diaries showed evidence of a need for help with the tasks a spouse would have performed. One sign of frustration in finding that help outside of a marital relationship is that some younger widowed diarists chose to remarry despite strong ambivalence. The need for substitutes was obvious in parent-child relationships. Parents turned to some extent to children for support and help, even when children could not provide it. Men needed help in caring for young dependent children; widows sometimes needed help with a child who had been controlled with physical threats and chastisement by the now dead father and husband.

The dynamics of family relationships, particularly between parents and children wrestling with the issue of substitution for the lost, seem to reflect another systems phenomenon, the interaction of griefs. The grief of one family member may complicate the attempts of others to turn to that person for help and understanding. Another expression of the interaction of griefs is conflict over inheritance. Although such disputes arise from many sources that have little to do with grief, they are intensified by the anger and needs stemming from the grief of each of the disputants.

A final systems phenomenon illuminated by some of the diaries is the role of help in grief. Diarists seemed to benefit from providing support to others. Offering help to others seemed to help some diarists deal with their own grief. Although diarists seemed to appreciate and benefit from the emotional support relatives and others provided, at times that support was a burden.

11

Amending the Theory of Grief Work and Other Theories

Although many theories deal with grief or can be used to understand it, much of the scholarly writing on the subject rests directly or indirectly on Freud's theory of grief work. The analyses in this book of grief in nineteenth-century diaries help clarify the theory and suggest amendments that embellish, qualify, or focus it. If one takes the outline of the theory of grief work presented in Chapter 3 as a first step how can the theory be clarified and amended in light of the findings and analyses presented elsewhere in this book?

As discussed in Chapter 2, the first diary entry reporting a loss was typically quite long, and often seemed to be an announcement of the onset of grief work. For "heavy" losses—losses of closely related household members—it was often the beginning of a sequence of obsessive entries that repeatedly returned to the same questions, the same examinations of the terminal illness and death and the same examinations of the diarist's dilemmas, problems, and feelings.

The Struggle

Discontinuity and Emotional Control

The struggle of grief work, as outlined in Chapter 3, involves the disconnecting of memories and hopes from the person who has been lost. After a brief initial period this struggle, as reported particularly in Chapters 6 and 9, is not continuous. People do not struggle constantly with their griefs (Bowlby, 1980, p. 231). In fact, one could even consider recurrent obsessive review in grief, which is sometimes taken as an indication of continuity in grieving, as a sign that the bereaved has backed away from the struggle since the last review. The review may be necessary because the bereaved is starting anew to define the problems created by the loss and their alternative solutions, and may have been out of contact with the facts, events, and issues that must be kept in mind while struggling with the situation.

One reason for the discontinuity, which seems to call for an amendment to the theory of grief work, is that people are disposed to control their emotions some of the time (cf. Glick, Weiss, & Parkes, 1974, p. 215; Parkes, 1972, pp. 87-88). To do this they often back away from the struggle of grief work by acting inconsistently with their feelings, by avoiding reminders of the loss, by self-instructing in a way that enables them to live in greater equanimity, or by finding ways to minimize the loss. Freud wrote about the energy absorbed by grief work, and it may be that people back away from grief work in order to save some of their energy for other tasks or to save themselves from exhaustion. The fact that several diarists said, in conjunction with their statements about emotional control, that they had to deal with their young children or their work could be taken to mean that emotional control allows energy expenditure for other tasks. People may also back away temporarily from grief work for the same reasons they might back away from any other combat — to get fresh perspective, to restore energy, or to heal wounds that are being rasped too painfully in the struggle.

From the perspective of the diaries, the ego defenses involved in the emotional control of grief are not necessarily maladaptive (cf. Glick, Weiss, & Parkes, 1974, pp. 215, 295-296; Parkes, 1972, p. 92). Although some writers on grief argue that a bereaved person's turning away from grief is a sign or a cause of pathology, such turning away seems to be normal (in the sense of being common), to be rarely associated with pathology, and to be typically a sign of coping. It seems that only the person who is isolated from others and lacks responsibilities or necessary daily chores can afford to devote all energy to grieving. Even then, such total devotion may make it relatively difficult to carry out necessary grief work, because the person will have more difficulty in acquiring fresh perspectives, in renewing personal energy, and in developing a life pattern that does not require the psychological presence of the person now lost. The fact that comparatively isolated people have more trouble coming to a state resembling an end of grieving (Clayton, 1975) supports this notion. It does not seem to be inconsistent with the theory of grief work, as represented in Freud's "Mourning and Melancholia," to argue for temporary withdrawal from grief work. Thus, it seems an appropriate amendment to the theory to state that people will typically withdraw at times, that this withdrawal is related to social and subsistence demands and perhaps to the demands of the grief work process itself, and that periodic withdrawal may facilitate grief work.

Cognitive Sources of Discontinuity

After the early part of the struggle, the bereaved will have dealt with many crucial aspects of the loss. But not all memories and hopes will be salient at any one time. This is another reason for discontinuity in grief work. Life is too complicated, memory too fallible, consciousness too limited in scope for a bereaved person to deal in a short time with all the memories and hopes that must eventually be dealt with. For this reason, the bereaved would resume the grief work struggle recurrently as fresh memories and hopes that have not yet been dealt with are encountered. Reminders are particularly important in this respect. Many of the stimuli to grieving listed in Chapter 2 are plausible as fresh reminders more or less out of the bereaved's control and capable of forcing the bereaved to face memories and hopes not dealt with previously. For example, dates, such as birthdays, anniversaries, and holidays that were special in the relationship with the lost cannot easily be dealt with in advance. Perhaps someone who is tolerant of pain and foresighted could think through, with calendar in hand, what each day in the coming year might signify and thereby carry out a substantial amount of grief work, but the trappings of some of the special days could still be unanticipated and come as reminders not yet dealt with—Christmas decorations, New Year's and July 4 celebrations by neighbors, and so on.

Significant family events such as a birth, a wedding, or a property loss may be difficult or impossible to anticipate early in bereavement. Each may bring with it a realization of what was lost that one could not have realized before (Johnson & Rosenblatt, 1981). The memory or hope was latent. An adult who has lost a parent could not anticipate, for example, the realization that her or his new child will lack a maternal grandmother. Or a widow could not anticipate that the dwelling shared with her deceased husband would burn and with it a sense of shared place that was part of her remaining connection with him. Similarly, an encounter with someone who looks like the lost, who mentions the lost, or who reminds one in some other way of the lost is also difficult to anticipate and might well tap memories and hopes not previously dealt with.

If it is granted that there are fresh reminders, that losses cannot be worked on all of a piece, it becomes plausible that normal grieving involves repeated surges of grief (Parkes, 1972, p. 57, called them "pangs"). It would be normal, then, for the bereaved to say something like what C. S. Lewis (1961, pp. 46-47) said in grieving for his wife, "How often—will it be for always?—how often will the vast emptiness astonish me like a complete novelty and make me say, 'I never realized my loss till this moment'?"

Since important reminders that set off fresh grieving are linked to an annual cycle of anniversaries, holidays, and other significant dates, one can expect recurrent grieving for any loss throughout the first year of bereavement. A rule of thumb that says grieving should be completed in less than a year seems inappropriate. In fact, if the life cycle guarantees that people recurrently encounter new events that remind them of persons lost to them, then for major losses one may never complete grief work (cf. Johnson & Rosenblatt, 1981).

Struggle and Gradual Retreat

In any struggle, one is unlikely to concede losses immediately, but will attempt to hold on to as much as one can. A struggle can be expected to involve a gradual retreat more often than instant surrender. Hence, it seems plausible, in fact normal, that early in grief one would try to hold on to more continuity with the time before the loss than one can eventually maintain. Some of the positions commonly taken during the slow retreat of grief work are discussed in Chapter 10. One's first reaction to a report of loss might be to doubt it. When doubt is no longer possible, one might next try to maintain one's world, as much as one can, as it was before the loss, experiencing a sense of presence of the lost, attempting to communicate with him or her, or trying to act on his or her wishes. One's next line of defense might be to try to make minimal substitutions for the lost, involving the least amount of change in one's pattern of living—for example, turning to God, a household member, or a relative as a substitute. Only in the long run would it be plausible, from the point of view of the dynamics of struggle, that one would make major changes, conceding the enormity of one's loss.

It seems appropriate, then, to add to the theory of grief work the amendment that the struggle does not involve random trial and error in adjusting to loss but follows a path of attempting the most conservative changes first. When these fail, one will move to less conservative positions. But it is only rather late in the grief work that one will make the major changes the situation calls for. From this perspective, initial adjustments to grief that seem unrealistic to an outsider can be understood as a sign of normal grief work, a sign that the bereaved is engaging in the struggle appropriately. What would be odd would be to concede all from the beginning.

The Time Course of Grief Work

The time course of grief for major losses is erratic, and the peaks of great grief may not be particularly predictable. Moreover, a good case can be made that grief for major losses never completely ends. Yet the surges of great grief, as the theory of grief work would seem to predict, tend to become less numerous after the initial weeks and months of bereavement.

The dynamics of grief work involve not only what goes on in a person's head, but also interactions with the environment. People who do not have to face reminders of the lost, who do not have to interact with others, and who do not have demanding tasks that must be done will make slow progress, if any, toward completing grief work. It is not a simple matter to walk into painful situations, and people will not necessarily do so if they need not. Thus, people in environments that demand action and those surrounded by reminders of the lost can be expected to carry out grief work most rapidly. Engaging in speedy grief work does not, of course, mean a person is experiencing little pain. On the contrary, there may be intense concentrations of pain.

Anticipation

The discussion, in Chapter 4, of anticipatory grief suggested that there have been substantial defects in all empirical analyses of anticipatory grief, but it also suggested that there are constraints on the grief work process. In comparing grief over deaths with grief over separations it was clear that the peace one makes with the person one will lose, saying goodbyes, and finishing business can be done more easily for some kinds of anticipated loss than for others. With separations and with deaths of people outside one's household, longer anticipation tends to be associated with decreased grief. Despite the similar effects of anticipation on grief for separation and grief for death of noncoresidents, what goes on during the anticipation period may be quite different for the two kinds of loss. With separations, longer anticipation seems to allow more time to make plans for communication or reunion and to define the separation as not reflecting negatively on the person from whom one is separating. In the case of the death of a noncoresident, the longer anticipation may allow for some anticipatory grief work; one is not pressed to continue one's interaction with the dying person. Coresidence seems to limit or prevent grief work before the loss, and care of the dying person during the terminal illness may actually add a rich store of additional memories and hopes to deal with during grief work.

Freud's statement of the theory of grief work does not deal with anticipatory grief. But much of the scholarly discussion of anticipatory grief seems to rest on the notion of grief work. To these discussions, several amendments are suggested. First, anticipatory grieving may not go on in the case of separation, even when anticipation may make it seem as though some grief work has already occurred. Second, it may be impossible, and certainly very difficult, to carry out anticipatory grieving while one is still in close contact with the person whose death is anticipated. The discussion in Chapter 4 also raised the possibility that many other factors will eventually have to be considered in amending the theory of grief work to accommodate anticipatory grief—factors such as certainty of prognosis, hope of cure, involvement in terminal care, and interactions between the dying person and the prospective bereaved during the anticipation periods.

Age and Response to Reminders

The discussion in Chapter 7 of differences during separation between leavers and left provided additional evidence for the effect of reminders on the initial struggles of grief work. The importance of coresidence in differentiating initial grieving by older people who were leavers and those who were left suggests that the reminders around one govern the initial intensity of the grief work struggle, particularly if one has already had some experience with grief. It may be that leavers and left will eventually have to struggle with the same things (though leavers may never encounter some reminders that people who were left have to deal with), but at least the grief work falls more heavily on older people who are left than on older leavers.

Younger diarists showed the same level of grief, a relatively high one, during the first month of separation whether they were the leaver or the left. Among older diarists, greater grief over separation occurred among the left, rather than the leaver, provided the diarist and the person from whom the diarist had separated were living together before the separation. The age difference suggests that among younger people any separation, perhaps any loss, will be rather strongly bereaving. These age effects, as suggested in Chapters 8 and 9, may arise from differences in learning to control grief and in the meaning of a loss, which may be more shocking for a younger person who has not yet come to grips with the inevitability of loss. In some cases, however, age differences may be counteracted by effects of duration of relationship. At least in the case of marriage, as indicated in Chapter 8, longer relationships may lead to stronger grief (cf. Marris, 1958, p. 35).

Dynamics of Memory and Hope

The theory of grief work does not give a sense of the way the grief work struggle is dependent on individual surroundings and experiences during bereavement. However, when one considers the dynamics of memory, it seems clear that whatever affects the normal memory process will affect the normal grief work process. Memories are stimulated by reminders, and reminders, as evidenced in the Chapter 9 discussion of emotional control and of difficult returnings, the Chapter 8 discussions of the effect of coresidence prior to death, and many other discussions in this book, give people more to work on and affect the frequency of expression of grief over time. The assertion that reminders have a crucial role in the dynamics of memory in grief work is offered as an amendment to the theory of grief work.

The comparison in Chapter 6 of the time courses of grief for deaths and for separations demonstrates that irreversible losses are dealt with rather effectively. In the long run, people grieve more for the living they cannot see and be with than for the dead, who can never return. The possibility of renewed contact makes relatively complete grief work impossible in the case of separation. In terms of the theory of grief work, two mechanisms may underlie the difference in reactions to deaths and separations. One can retain hope if the loss is due to separation; thus, at least some hopes cannot be disposed of in the grief work process. Also, communication during separation may mean that memories are more often jogged in separation than in death, and that new memories continue to be created. Thus, grief work on memories will go more slowly for separations than for deaths.

Finally, the discussion in Chapter 8 suggested a different time course for grief work on memories than on hopes. From data on grief over the deaths of children of different ages, it seems that one confronts hopes much more at the beginning. The first grief work struggles are concentrated relatively heavily on hopes. Subsequently, memories are dealt with more. Thus, the time course of grief over a relationship built largely on hopes may be in some sense a shorter one, but grief may also be relatively intense at first. The time course of grief over a relationship with rich memory stores may or may not be relatively intense at first, but it will last much longer, and quite possibly as long as one lives.

Developmental Theories, Symbolic Interaction Theory and Memory Theories

As well as offering suggestions and amendments for the theory of grief work, this book provides perspective on a number of other theories, among them developmental theories (both individual and family), symbolic interaction theory, and theories of memory.

At the level of individual development, the findings of the research reported here suggest that development is still occurring well into adulthood if one has not experienced a major grief until then. The first major losses experienced seem to produce more intense bereavement. This seems to be due to an underdeveloped capacity for emotional control and probably to facing one's own mortality and that of the people around one more realistically. Responses to subsequent losses presumably reflect a greater capacity for self-control and a sense that, however horrible it may be, other people die and one will also die. A clearer set of beliefs and understandings about death and a more organized and clear sense of what to do when death occurs may also be developing.

From the point of view of family development theory (Hill & Rodgers, 1964), the diary data discussed in Chapter 10 suggest that in the case of a major loss due to death, individuals and families do not move abruptly into another family stage. Rather, there is a liminal (or threshold) period (cf. van Gennep, 1960) during which a struggle occurs to maintain the old developmental stage, and new realistic role allocations have not yet been made.

Symbolic interaction theory (e.g., Brissett & Edgley, 1975; also see Marris, 1974, for a symbolic interactionist analysis of grief) focuses in part on definitions of the situation. It asserts, among many things, that people prefer to have stable definitions of the situation they are in, and by and large they live with such stability. But the data reported here on recurrent surges of grief suggest that in bereavement one has difficulty hanging on to a stable definition of the situation. Even when one thinks one has achieved some sort of peace, one may subsequently experience intense grief. The sense of instability that would arise from repeated failure to sustain the peace one believes one has achieved must add distress to one's grief.

Symbolic interaction theory also deals with the importance of others in defining ourselves and our situations. When somebody important to one dies, one loses definitions of self and situations that came out of interaction with that person. The different responses of people who were leavers and those who were left suggest that the definitional problems may be greater for the person who was left. This person has to wrestle with the incongruence between the familiarity of the situation and the strangeness of definitions of situation and self. The leaver is in a strange situation but does not have the incongruence problem. Instead, the leaver expects to deal with novelty and perhaps to generate new definitions.

From the viewpoint of symbolic interaction theory it seems reasonable that living together should make a difference in bereavement reactions. The theory weighs daily interactions heavily as factors influencing sense of self and of reality (Berger & Kellner, 1964; Rosenblatt & Wright, unpublished). It is not simply an abstract relationship—say, one of parent and child—that gives sense of self and situation, although one can credit some of one's current sense of self and situation to one's history of interaction. Rather, it is the day-to-day interactions that operate crucially. Thus, the loss of a coresident means that, in addition to all one's other losses, one loses important interactions that help define one's sense of self and of reality.

The diary data on emotional control can also be thought of in terms of symbolic interaction theory. People control their emotions by redefining a situation to focus on something other than loss, by defining the loss as not so bad or as counterbalanced by gains, by making plans or instructing themselves in a way that demonstrates a nonbereaved or less bereaved definition of self and situation, and by avoiding reminders of the incongruence between the former and current definitions of the situation and of self.

The emotional control material and the material on leaver vs. left, on recurrent grief, and on the time course of grief work all suggest principles for a theory of memory. There are experimental psychology theories of memory, theories dealing with factors affecting recall, recognition, and the organization of memories (e.g. Kintsch, 1970). Studying something as unpredictable and long-term as the time course of grief seems outside the scope of current laboratory-based memory work, yet the concept of "cue" or reminder has a long history in work on memory. It seems obvious that work on the grief process would gain from studies of memory in everyday life. The findings reported in this book suggest some of the memory phenomena to probe more closely. It may be possible, for example, to predict more clearly when grief will resurge, when emotional control will break down, and when the bereaved will be inclined to face reminders that have been avoided.

What Can Be Believed?

For a person who would rather doubt than believe the findings and tentative conclusions of this study there is much justification. Diarists may be odd; the diaries may have been censored; the "sampling" procedures engaged in by archivists, publishers of diaries, and the researcher provide no assurance that a representative sample of diarists has been studied. Moreover, the quantitative analyses reported here count losses, not diarists, a process that some would consider to undermine their claims to validity (see Appendix C). The theory of grief work seemed applicable to the nineteenth-century diary materials, because the diaries contained much material that the theory would lead one to expect. The findings from the diaries match well with those from major studies of grief such as those of Parkes (1972) and of Glick, Weiss, and Parkes (1974). A skeptic would not have granted that in advance and, given the opportunistic sample, might still not grant it in the face of what has been reported here.

In any era, attachments between people may be quite diverse. And comparison of nineteenth- and twentieth-century attachments may show many differences that could invalidate the use of information about nineteenth-century relationships to provide insight into twentieth-century relationships. Historical researchers have found variability across time and place in factors that could influence people's close relationships or their reactions to the termination of those relationships—factors like household composition, age at marriage, and mode of disciplining children. So one can never be certain that it is valid to use nineteenth-century material to develop twentieth-century relationship theories. Moreover, diaries are in many ways a flimsy foundation for knowledge. The relationship between what people say in their diaries and what would appear to an outsider to be going on in their lives may be tenuous, and there may be no way to verify most of what diarists say about their feelings. Nonetheless, the fact that similarities exist in the diary data supports the assumption that the diaries of diverse people from different periods in a complicated century are of value in the development of theories of bereavement. Ultimately, this work must be judged on the basis of its usefulness in understanding and dealing with grief.

Appendixes

Appendix A
Working with Diaries

Ethical Issues in Studying Diaries

In an era of voyeurism in the name of science, in which people's most intimate relationships and thoughts may be reported to the public, one may not feel any compunction about studying the diary of another. However, most of the diaries in the public domain were put there not by the diarists, but by their descendants, by literary executors, or by some stranger who happened on the diary in an attic or at an estate sale. Many diarists whose writings are used in this book gave no sense that they were thinking of possible future readers, and of those who did, most did so only occasionally or as an afterthought. To make the ethical implications of working with diaries clearer, here are some diary passages referring to possible future readers. In the following entries from seven different diaries, the diversity of wishes, expectations, and imaginings about possible readers suggests that the ethical thing to do would be different from diary to diary.

In the first of the series of diary entries, I. O. Krohnke seems to be writing for the public, at least in some places in his diary. Archibald Gillies and Sally Squire are aware that their diaries may become public, though the former hopes that his or a reader's standard of decency may preclude the publication of some material, and the latter hopes that the reader will profit (by her standards, one assumes) through the reading of the diary.

* * * * * * *

"The readers of my diary probably will ask, does this belong in a diary? I do not believe this myself and ask to excuse myself . . ." (August 18, 1848). "If this diary is going to be read by people also leaving their home and trying to find a new home across they should learn from my experience and not take any hired workers over . . ." (February 5, 1849).

Diary of I. O. Krohnke, a Wisconsin farmer from Germany, unpublished typescript translation, State Historical Society of Wisconsin. For more complete biographical and bibliographical information on Krohnke and other diarists, see Appendix B.

* * *

"If my time here on this fair Universe be exhausted before the end of this book be reached, may some kind friend please preserve it, or if there be anything within the covers that would bring shame upon he or she who may try to do such, may it be committed to the flames. . . . May those who may chance at intervals to glance over the different pages please refrain from mentioning at the time any such thing which should not become the property of the public. . . ."

Diary of Archibald Gillies, unpublished manuscript, Archives of Ontario, entry of March 1, 1893. A school teacher in Temperanceville, Ontario, Gillies was 23 when he wrote this passage at the beginning of a new volume of his diary.

* * *

"I did not write this little book with a view to have it exposed to the world. . . . So fearful have I been that some one should read this, that I have concealed it in my absence. But I calculate now, as I am about to close my book, to let my nearest earthly friend only peruse it at his leisure and God grant it may be of service to both of us. . . . As my life is uncertain this pamphlet may be read by many and perhaps ridiculed by some, but that does not discourage me if I could be assured that one soul would profit by it, I should be amply rewarded. . . ."

Diary of Sally Squire, unpublished manuscript, Manuscripts and Archives Division, New York Public Library, Astor, Lenox, and Tilden Foundations, entry of July 9, 1816.

* * *

"With the closing year this book comes to an end & the question arises shall this be destroyed and thus share the fate of several of its predecessors, or shall I keep it so that my children may after my death see some of the exercises of their Mothers mind? If I thought that I were actuated by a desire that my friends should know after my death what I feared to speak of now, I would instantly destroy it.

"Were it not for the sake of my children, I would never save any of the exercises of my mind which sometimes I am obliged to note down, by some irresistible impulse; but the hope of doing them some little good, has influenced me to preserve some of the sketches of the different states of my mind during the last few years. Previous to that I used to write very much more than I now do, but at the beginning of every New Year destroy all that I had retained during the year. But this I will preserve, at least for a while, as it may serve for amusement & be of some benefit to me when ill & feeble by recalling the mercies of the Lord in times past.

"Another motive is that after I am taken away my dear children may have some knowledge of the *many, many* times which I have devoted to prayers 'with strong cries and tears,' for them & perhaps they may then be induced to consecrate themselves wholly to the service of the Lord. . . ."

Last entry of last diary volume of Mary White, unpublished manuscript, Huntington Library, entry of December 30, 1855.

* * *

"May this journal, to our children impart
The truths of their mothers inmost heart;
May they peruse its contents with delight;
Aye, like its author, may they strive to do right.
Eighteen long years have passed away
Since I commenced to keep a diary;
Alas! All things are not just what they seem.
Yet, this life of ours seems but a passing dream.
Then, a happy school-girl no thought or care.
Aye; of those years agone, memories are dear:
Now with our innocent little ones, it may be
The brightest hour, Lord we commend ourselves to thee."

Diary of Emily Hawley Gillespie, undated poem from page one of book seven, 1875-1878, unpublished manuscript, Iowa State Historical Society, Iowa City.

* * *

"I wonder at myself when I look at my *ten years' Diaries* — labor in accomplishing a mass of nothings — scrawls which, if saved, even for garret-furniture, will soon molder to dust. However, in my weakness, I have taken some pleasure in this pen-service, of 3650 written dates, without the omission of one day, notwithstanding some serious seasons of sickness and accidents. Through them all, Heaven has enabled me to write a few lines each day — numbering in all more than 74,000! But, alas! — what are they worth? Still I shall not destroy them. They are my only legacy to my family, poor as they may be in sentiment and phrase. . . ."

Diary of Thomas Edmonds, unpublished manuscript, Huntington Library, December 31, 1849, age 69.

* * *

"These lines are pened [sic] that in after life should my life be spared I may have the opportunity of comparing myself with myself, & of calling to mind many events which might be forgotten. By looking over this I am reminded of the different situations in which I have been placed and the kind of thoughts I then had. It is intended exclusively for my own use & many things are mentioned which to any one but myself must appear extremly [sic] trifling; yet they are linked with associations which to me are interesting.

"As life is uncertain I write this page that should I be taken away sudenly [sic], this book may not be seen except by a sister or some very near and intimate friend, & I hope that my friend will have the compassion to burn it immediately. Should it by chance fall into the hands of any other, pray be so good as not to read it."

Diary of Mary Richardson Walker—on the first page of the earliest extant portion of her diary, dated January 1, 1833, p. 21 of published volume (M. Walker, 1963).

* * * * * * *

If one observed an ethical injunction to respect people's wishes or to allow them the privacy they desire, one would not use the diaries of White, Gillespie, Edmonds, or Walker at all, and one would be very careful in using the diaries of both Gillies and Squire. One would attempt to learn what Gillies considered information that should be suppressed and what Squire considered "profit" in the use of her diary and try to adhere to their standards. But as with any ethical question, there are other positions.

One could argue that the dead have no rights, and that the rights of the living should always prevail over any wish or injunction issued by a person now dead. I am quite uncomfortable with that position, though it may be a predominant one in western culture. My preference is that the diaries of people living or dead be treated with respect and sensitivity, by both my standards and theirs. But it is also my preference that the diaries of people long dead be available to the living to help them to live better, to understand their own lives better, to live with less pain and more enlightenment. From that point of view, it is legitimate to use a person's diary to help one understand one's own griefs and the griefs of others, but we owe it to the diarists to take their understandings of things seriously, to avoid ridiculing them, and (one reason I use nineteenth-century diaries) to avoid disclosing the contents of their diaries to people who knew them. Thus, in my thinking, people long dead count just as much as the living, but I feel more willingness to use their diaries because I will not be disclosing any diary contents to people who knew them and whose opinions counted with the diarist. Although I have the option of disguising my sources by presenting nothing but statistical summaries or quotes without identification, I think there is too much richness in the diary passages to omit them and too much value in observing the canons of scholarship to ignore those canons.

Diaries Are Not Necessarily What One Would Assume Them to Be

The ideal diary provides a daily, private personal record, without censorship and without distortion arising from concern about someone else's reading it. The ideal diary delves deeply into the diarist's consciousness, reporting inner feelings, hidden thoughts, dreams, the inner dialogue, the illogical, and the fantastic. But if one looks at published diaries or those in public archives, they almost invariably deviate from the ideal.

Most diaries seem to be centered on a single theme or a small handful of themes. The favorite themes seem to be the weather, major chores, travels, church events, visiting, correspondence, major family occurrences (births, deaths, major property losses, marriages, christenings), neighborhood events (a fire, a flood, the opening of the railroad, the establishment of a telegraph link with the outside world), or national news (the assassination of a President, the onset of a war). Diaries are most often not introspective. They are simply superficial, laconic memos. Occasionally a major event may alter a theme, or a long gap in diary keeping may precede the onset of a new theme. Deaths of people close to the diarist are one of the sources of a change in theme, though sometimes a death of a parent, spouse, or child leads to the ending of diary keeping (cf. Fothergill, 1974, p. 14). Diaries rich in words about the inner life are rare. Whether that means that people are rarely introspective is unclear. Many diarists lacked the economic resources to write much—they hadn't the paper, the ink, or perhaps the time. Many seemed interested only in listing memoranda of things that had happened. Farmers, for example, may have wanted a record of weather as a guide to future planting and harvesting.

Perhaps many diarists were careful about what they wrote because they had no guarantee of privacy. A diary that appeared to be very interesting to a diarist might become interesting to people around the diarist. In the nineteenth century and perhaps even now, many people lacked a secure place for personal items. Moreover, in the United States and Canada in the nineteenth century (the locus of the sample in this study), women's rights to privacy often seem to have been put aside if a mature (or at least older) male in the household felt it was appropriate. There are four diaries in the sample in which the diarist's wall of privacy is clearly though temporarily breached. In every case, the diarist is a comparatively young female and the invader a male (spouse, older brother, or landlord). Here are quotes touching on each instance in the sample.

* * * * * * *

"Charles was reading my diary of yesterday. . . . I told him to stop arguing and to stop reading my diary. . . ."

Diary of Mary Alice Shutes Mallory (Mallory, 1967). Mallory was age 13 at the time of the entry, May 27, 1862. Charles was her brother.

* * *

"To Rev. E. Walker

"My dear husband I find it in vain to expect my Journal will escape your eyes & indeed why should I wish to have it [so]? Certainly my mind knows no sweeter solace than the privilege of unbosoming itself to you. It frequently happens that when I think of much I wish to say to you, you are either so much fatigued, so drowsy or so busy that I find no convenient opportunity till what I would have said is forgotten. I have therefore determined to address my journal to you. I shall at all times address you with the unrestrained freedom of a fond & confiding wife. When therefore you have leisure & inclination to know my heart, you may here find it ready for converse."

Diary of Mary Richardson Walker (1963, p. 164), entry of July 26, 1839.

"Have felt the past week several times as if I could no longer endure certain things that I find in my husband. I find it difficult to obtain relief on a subject like this. For I cannot speak of him—nor to him—& if I write I fear he will read. . . ."

Diary of Mary Richardson Walker (1963, p. 197), entry of August 23, 1840.

* * *

"Mr. Bissell was standing in the vestibule looking so nice, doubtless was disappointed at not seeing Mrs. L. [the diarist]" Mrs. L. is a widow at this entry date. The next paragraph of the entry begins, "The above was written by Mr. Kolb [the diarist's landlord] who is a joking, dear old fellow."

Diary of Dolly Lunt Burge (1962, p. 27), entry for April 15, 1849. Mr. Bissell had been courting the diarist.

* * *

Written in different handwriting, vertically across the day's entry: "I hereby [?] these remarks. I think Nell is one grand Humbugery—I do." The entry of the diarist reads, in part, "Henry has been scolding me for several things—Faux pas which I make. I suppose he is quite mortified sometimes. He thinks I don't know how to act at all & that I am a fool. . . . He is looking over my shoulders & eave droppers never hear any good of themselves."

Diary of Nellie Wetherbee, unpublished manuscript, Bancroft Library, University of California, Berkeley, entry of September 12, 1860.

* * * * * * *

Obviously women could not always count on males in their households to honor the privacy of a diary, but what motivated the males is uncertain. Was it simple curiosity or an urge to dominate? Since some women (e.g., Mary Richardson Walker and Nellie Wetherbee) used their diaries as vehicles for the expression of marital disillusionment, it is possible that the association of signs of anger or sorrow with diary writing made the diary especially interesting to a husband who found it difficult to understand his wife.

Even when a female diarist thought her diary had not been looked at by the man in her life, she might have been aware of the possibility. For example: "Now, if By [the diarist's husband] were to see this, he would make sport of me, but he never looks into this Journal, I'm sure." Diary of Mollie Dorsey Sanford (1959, p. 142), undated entry written in August or September, 1860.

There were some diarists who intended to show their writing to someone, not merely as an afterthought or occasional speculation (as was the case with White, Gillespie, and Edmonds quoted above) but as an intention reflected in virtually every entry. Here are some examples from the diaries of Elisabeth Koren (1955) and Elkanah Walker (1976).

* * * * * * *

From the diary of Elisabeth Koren (1955):

"He . . . reads my diary to learn how I have fared while he was away" (p. 143), entry of January 24, 1854.

"Vilhelm was reading my diary, which is one of the first things he does when he gets home . . ." (p. 185), entry of March 7, 1854.

"Now all of Saturday, Sunday, and Monday have passed without my doing any writing; this is too bad! I believe it is because Vilhelm is home; when he is, I never care as much about writing as when he is away. Then I always regret not having written, for I know he is eager to read what I write. Since he is to start out tomorrow, we shall see if the inclination returns" (p. 207), entry of April 4, 1854.

"I shall now try to write a little, in the hope that I may be left in peace by Vilhelm. He is very naughty and has been teasing me all forenoon. While we were eating breakfast, he was still quite good-natured. I had been up fairly early and set the table and had everything ready by the time my lazy husband was finally dressed. (He really made his bed, too, Papa.) [The interpolations in parentheses in this paragraph are in Pastor Koren's handwriting in the diary.] As I stated, while we were eating, everything was lovely. . . . Vilhelm was so mean and naughty that I became angry and tried a dozen ways to make him be quiet. (She struck me, P.) . . . Then I also had to hear that I was cross and ill-behaved. Yes, we have heavy afflictions, alas, not least at the hands of our spouses. This I surely experienced today; nor was it the first time. (She became angriest of all because, when she insisted that no woman's name ended in 'us', I answered by naming 'Rasmus.') [. . . 'Rasmus' is a colloquial term in Norwegian for a nagging, scolding wife.] At last I tired of him and sat down to write; this brought about a temporary truce . . ." (p. 237), entry of June 14, 1854.

"'Is that all you have to say about this day?' Vilhelm will remark when he reads this. 'Can't you really keep your mind on anything but the work you have in hand?' . . ." (p. 253), entry of June 23, 1854.

"Tonight I am tired, too, but first I must nevertheless tell my diary—or rather him who reads the diary—that I am so well pleased I almost forgot my tiredness . . ." (p. 254), entry of June 30, 1854.

"Yesterday, too, we had a cozy time. Vilhelm read my diary and letters" (p. 268), entry of July 12, 1854.

". . . we had coffee and talked, giving each other an account of the time we had been separated. Vilhelm read my diary" (p. 294), entry of August 3, 1854.

"I suppose I ought not write this—when Vilhelm reads it, he will say I am careless and the like. But I have now told it to him just the same . . ." (p. 297), entry of August 5, 1854.

"Vilhelm will want to scold me when he reads this; I am not supposed to be so fainthearted, or whatever I should call it. . . . It is a long time since I last wrote here—almost a week now, I believe. That is always a sign that Vilhelm has been home . . ." (pp. 340-341), entry of November 11, 1854.

* * *

"I am writing this while brother E. is in bed & fast to sleep. I take much delight in writing this journal because my dear companion will read it with pleasure. It is for her sake that I write more than for my own gratification."

Diary of Elkanah Walker (1976, p. 75), entry of September 18, 1838. Walker was on a trip and kept a special journal to share with his wife. The journal he wrote at other times seems to have been only for himself.

* * * * * * *

Several diarists, while temporarily incapacitated, dictated entries to a spouse or grown offspring. Sometimes a diarist showed an entry or several entries to a friend or relative. Mollie Dorsey Sanford, for example, reported that a newly made friend "has had a peep at my journal. I wonder if she has seen my comments about herself. She knows I love her" (1959, p. 8, entry of April 5, 1857).

In addition, there are examples, such as those quoted in the discussion of the ethics of studying diaries, of diarist thoughts about possible invasions of privacy. White, Gillespie, and Edmonds all wondered, in the course of diary keeping, whether the diary might be read by their children; Gillies and Squire realized that they might not be able to prevent others from reading their diaries. All these examples indicate that there may have been strong reasons for diarists to censor their entries.

Much of the censorship may have left no trace. The diarist may merely have neglected to report some thought. But occasionally a diarist did leave a record of censorship. White, in a passage quoted above, indicated that she discarded diary volumes. Squire's diary, which was also quoted above, and the diaries of William H. Brisbane and Thomas Mills Day had pages torn out—perhaps by the diarist. (Some of the apparent censorship may have been performed by spouses, friends, or descendants of the diarists.) The diaries of some people in the sample contain erasures, passages pasted over others, and entries referring to "rewriting" or "copying over." Some diarists occasionally used a code or wrote parts of some entries in a foreign language. (Many of these instances seem to have been records of menstrual periods.) All these indications of possible censorship by the diarists suggest that relatively few diaries contain an ideal, uncensored account of the diarist's inner life.

The ideal diary would also have daily entries, but many diaries do not contain daily entries for substantial stretches of time. Even when there are entries for each day, some diarists indicated here and there that some entries were actually written days, weeks, or even months after the dates given for them. One wonders how many entries were made a substantial time after their dates without any hint that such is the case. Thus, even though diaries give a much finer texture of report than an account written at one time, they do not necessarily give an uncensored daily record, even when they appear to. All in all, if one wanted to work only with ideal diaries, a large majority of diaries would have to be ignored and most, perhaps all, of the rest would be suspect.

Coding Grief and Mentions of the Lost

All data coding for this book was done by the author. As a check on the reliability of the codings of mentions of the lost and of grief, materials were examined from each of 10 randomly chosen diarists in the sample. For each diarist dealing with more than one death, the specific loss to be used in the reliability analysis was also chosen randomly. Independent codings were made by Sandra Titus. Her count of number of mentions of the lost agreed perfectly with the author's for 98% of the months (a count could be made for each loss for up to 36 months). Her count of number of mentions with grief agreed for 99% of the months. The cases of disagreement were usually discrepant by only a single mention or a single mention with grief.

The key measures used in statistical analyses in this book are of proportion of monthly entries that contain mentions of the specific lost person and proportion of monthly entries that contain grief for the specific lost person. To attempt to measure intensity of grief seemed too risky; it is too difficult to know whether one person's simple "alas" is actually expressive of less grief than another person's multipage lament. Even in counting proportion of entries with grief, it must be assumed that a person who expressed grief in one entry out of five in a month experienced more grief than a person who expressed grief in one entry out of 30 or in no entry among three in a month. In the ultimate analysis, the value of the measures of grief must rest on the plausibility of the accounts and the agreement of findings reported here with personal experiences, theory, and past and future research findings. The fact of high agreement between another coder and the author provides some reassurance that however faulty the diary data are, the quantitative analyses reflect a creditable job of counting whatever is in the diaries.

Appendix B
The Diarists

This appendix lists each person whose diary was tabulated in analyses reported in this monograph, the source(s) from which the diary was obtained, the dates of entries contributing data (including background information and quotations), the numbers of deaths and separations that were tabulated from the diary, and the relationship of the diarist to any other diarist.

Anderson, Thomas Gummersall. Source: Anderson Papers, Canadian History Department, Metropolitan Toronto Central Library. Diary entries used for the years 1858 and 1859. One death.

Armstrong, Alfred F. Source: Diaries Collection, Archives of Ontario, Toronto. Diary for the years 1862-1863. One death.

Baldwin, Elijah. Source: Miscellaneous Diaries Collection, Sterling Memorial Library, Yale University. Diary entries used were for the years 1810-1815. One death.

Brisbane, P. Adeline (married surname Reed). Source: William Henry Brisbane Papers, State Historical Society of Wisconsin, Madison. Diaries for 1857-1858, 1864-1878, 1880-1882. Three deaths, two separations. P. Adeline was William Brisbane's daughter.

Brisbane, William H. Source: William Henry Brisbane Papers, State Historical Society of Wisconsin, Madison. Diary entries from 1834 to his death in 1878. Twelve deaths, 55 separations. William was P. Adeline Brisbane's father.

Burbank, August Ripley. Source: Filmed copy at Bancroft Library, University of California, Berkeley. Entries used for 1849-1851, 1853, 1880. One death, one separation.

Burge, Dolly Lunt. Source: Burge (1962), spanning the years 1847 (or possibly 1848) to 1879. Quoted material reprinted by permission of the University of Georgia Press. Six deaths.

Carleton, Thomas P. Source: Miscellaneous Diaries Collection, Sterling Memorial Library, Yale University, for the years 1867-1875, 1880-1881. Two deaths.

Carpenter, Mrs. Charles C. (Feronica Nancy Rice). Source: Film copy, Public Archives of Canada, Ottawa, Permission to quote granted by Thomas R. Carpenter, Tequesta, Florida. Material used for the years 1862 and 1863. Two deaths, one separation.

Cheever, Dustin G. Source: Dustin G. Cheever papers, Whitewater Manuscript Collection, State Historical Society of Wisconsin. Entries spanning the years 1851-1893. Two deaths, three separations.

Cleaveland, Elisha Lord. Source: The Cleaveland Papers, Sterling Memorial Library, Yale University. Entries used from 1856, 1860, 1863 to the diarist's death in 1866. One death.

Croswell, Harry. Source: Harry Croswell Papers, Sterling Memorial Library, Yale University. Entries for the period 1821-1857. Eight deaths.

Day, Thomas Mills. Source: Day Family Collection, Sterling Memorial Library, Yale University. Entries used for 1865 and 1866. One death.

Dent, Thomas. Source: Chicago Historical Society. Entries used for the period 1875-1878, 1880-1892. Four deaths, one separation.

Dodd, Mrs. William B. Source: Dodd Papers, Minnesota Historical Society, St. Paul. Diary for 1862-1863. One death.

Drew, Edward Bolivar. Source: James M. Drew and Family Papers, Minnesota Historical Society, St. Paul. Entries for the period 1859-1876. Four deaths, one separation.

Drinkwater, Sarah Hallen. Source: Diaries Collection, Archives of Ontario, Toronto. Entries used for 1841, 1864-1867. One death. Drinkwater was the sister of Eleanora Hallen.

Durrie, George H. Source: Miscellaneous Diaries Collection, Sterling Memorial Library, Yale University. Entries used for 1845-1846. Two deaths, three separations.

Edmonds, Thomas. Source: Huntington Library, San Marino, California. Entries used from 1844-1845, 1849. Three deaths, five separations.

Egbert, Eliza Ann (McAuley). Source: Filmed manuscripts, Bancroft Library, University of California, Berkeley. Entries for 1852. One separation.

Ely, Louise C. Foot. Source: Charles A. Ely Papers, Ohio Historical Society, Columbus. Entries for 1865-1867. Two deaths, one separation.

Fleming, Sir Sanford. Source: Fleming Papers, Archives of Ontario, Toronto. Entries for 1850-1854, 1866-1867. Two deaths.

Gillespie, Emily Hawley, Source: Sarah Gillespie Huftalen Collection, Iowa State Historical Department, State Historical Society of Iowa, Iowa City, Diary entries from 1861 to 1888. Two deaths, 12 separations.

Gillies, Archibald L. Source: Archives of Ontario, Toronto. Entries for 1888-1891, 1893-1896. Two deaths.

Gunn, Marcus. Source: Public Archives of Canada, Ottawa. Entries from 1819 to 1856. Twelve deaths, 24 separations.

Hallen, Eleanora. Source: Diaries Collection, Archives of Ontario, Toronto. Entries for 1845 and 1846. One separation. Hallen was the sister of Sarah Hallen Drinkwater.

Hempstead, Stephen. Source: Hempstead (1956, 1957, 1958, 1959, 1965, 1966), Diary entries spanning the years 1811 to 1831. Nineteen deaths.

Huntington, Susan Mansfield. Source: The John Trumbull Papers, Sterling Memorial Library, Yale University. Diary entries for 1819 to 1823. Three deaths, one separation.

Johnson, William. Source: Microfilmed transcript, Archives of Ontario, Toronto. Entries for 1832-1836, 1838-1841, 1847-1850. Three deaths, one separation.

Keyser, Linka. Source: Keyser (1952). Entries spanning the years 1844-1864. Two deaths, 12 separations.

Koren, Elisabeth. Source: Koren (1955). Entries for the years 1853-1855. Seven separations.

Krohnke, I. O. Source: State Historical Society of Wisconsin, Madison. Entries for 1848-1850. One death, one separation.

Lake, William B. Source: Bancroft Library, University of California, Berkeley. Entries for 1852-1854, 1856. One death, five separations.

Leith, George. Source: Microfilm typescript, Archives of Ontario, Toronto. Entries for 1834-1852. Three deaths, six separations.

Lovick, Sophia. Source: Privately held diary loaned by Rosalie Norem, Ames, Iowa. Entries for 1894-1899. One death.

Mallory, Mary Alice Shutes, Source: Mallory (1967). Entries for 1862. One separation.

Matthews, Richard F. Source: Canadian History Department, Metropolitan Toronto Central Library. Entries used for 1881-1889, 1892-1898. Five deaths, one separation.

Phillips, Martin W. Source: Phillips (1909). Entries used for 1840, 1846-1847, 1853-1855, 1857, 1859-1863. One death, one separation.

Sanderson, William F. Source: Typescript at Bancroft Library, University of California, Berkeley. Diary for 1863 and 1864. Two separations.

Sanford, Mollie Dorsey. Source: Sanford (1959). Diary entries spanning the years 1857-1866. Three deaths, six separations.

Scadding, Henry. Source: Canadian History Department, Metropolitan Toronto Central Library. Entries for 1833, 1841, 1843-1849, 1866. Two deaths.

Smith, Larratt. Source: Canadian History Department, Metropolitan Toronto Central Library. Entries for 1850-1856. Two deaths, two separations.

Snow, Corwin R. Source: Special Collections Dept., State University of Iowa Libraries, Iowa City. Entries used for 1894-1898. Three deaths.

Squire, Sally. Source: Manuscripts and Archives Division, New York Public Library, Astor, Lenox, and Tilden Foundations. Entries for 1815-1816. One death.

Udell, John. Source: Journal of John Udell. Los Angeles: Kovach, 1946, originally published in 1868. Entries for 1858-1859. One separation.

Walker, Elkanah. Sources: E. Walker (1976), and the Huntington Library, San Marino, California. Diary entries spanning the years 1838-1848. One death, two separations. Elkanah was Mary Richardson Walker's husband.

Walker, Mary Richardson. Sources: M. Walker (1963) and the Huntington Library, San Marino, California. Diary entries spanning the years 1833-1848. Two deaths, three separations. Mary was Elkanah Walker's wife.

Ward, Harriet Sherrill. Source: Typescript at the Bancroft Library, University of California, Berkeley. Diary entries for an overland trip in 1853. Three separations.

Ward, Lester. Source: Ward (1935). Diary entries spanning 1860-1869. Two deaths, three separations.

Washburn, Catherine Amanda Stansbury. Source: Quoted by permission of the Bancroft Library, University of California, Berkeley. Diary entries for 1853 overland trip. One separation.

Wetherbee, Nellie. Source: Quoted by permission of the Bancroft Library, University of California, Berkeley. Diary entries for 1860. One separation.

White, Mary A. Sources: Edited typescript provided by Kirk Jeffrey, Carleton College, Northfield, Minnesota, and original at the Huntington Library, San Marino, California. Entries spanning the years 1840-1855. Four deaths.

Wood, Sophia Sewell. Source: Miscellaneous Diaries Collection, Sterling Memorial Library, Yale University. Entries spanning the years 1809-1811. Two deaths.

Woodward, Mary Dodge. Source: Woodward (1937). Entries for the years 1884 through 1889. One death (her dog), seven separations.

Wright, George. Source: Public Archives of Canada, Ottawa. Entries for 1872, 1879. One death.

Wright, William W. Source: Typescript at State Historical Society of Wisconsin, Madison. Entries for 1841. One death.

Appendix C
On Statistics

Although there are a number of quantitative analyses in this book, there are no inferential statistics: statistics that assess the likelihood that some difference between proportions, some correlation, some pattern of correlations, or some other quantitative indicator deviates from what could occur by chance. Inferential statistics are valued by some people, if only because they help to evaluate whether some pattern of data is likely to be a chance variation from what would occur if the numbers were generated randomly (Winch & Campbell, 1969). There are, however, a number of reasons for not using inferential statistics.

The data of the present study violate assumptions of commonly used statistics and of the conditions that many people consider necessary for statistical inference to be valid. The cases were not randomly sampled from a defined universe. Analyses were done on numbers of losses rather than on numbers of diarists, but the losses are not independent of one another. The same idiosyncratic dynamics (the same personality, religious values, and so on) underlie the way losses were dealt with by a given diarist. When data are analyzed on a month-by-month or year-by-year basis, the separate months and separate years are not independent of one another; each month and each year reflects the uniqueness of the same diarists. Trend analyses could take that nonindependence into account, but such analyses are harder to do and to interpret when there are missing data, as there are in the diary material — people made entries in some months but not in others, and in some years but not in others, for most losses.

The violations of statistical assumptions are certainly a barrier to carrying out statistical inference procedures, but other factors argue even more strongly against performing statistical tests. One factor is that statistical tests make whatever one writes less accessible to a person without sophistication in statistics. Although that may not be a problem in a work that deals with relatively esoteric scientific issues, the present book deals with issues of importance to everybody, using materials that many people will find relevant to their own lives and easy to understand. It seems inappropriate, therefore, to block access to the material by embedding the findings in statistical analyses. Nonetheless, correlational analyses are offered in this appendix to bolster assertions made at several places in the book. The correlations are used descriptively, to show whether as values on one variable increase (e.g., duration of anticipatory period) values on another variable increase (e.g., proportion of diary entries in a given month that contain grief). The correlation coefficient summarizes whether, across all the cases, the more there is of one thing, the more there is of another. Values of the correlation coefficient can range from 1.00 through .00 to minus 1.00. A positive value means that the more there is of one thing, the more there is of another. A negative value means that the more there is of one thing, the less there is of another. A value of .00 means there is not even a shadow of a relationship between the two variables.

The reluctance to use inferential statistics also reflects a fear that they might be relied on in a way that would make theoretical issues less salient (cf. Bakan, 1966; Lykken, 1968). Researchers who use inferential statistics or the people who read their reports at times tend to follow the numbers rather than keeping track of the underlying theoretical issues. In the spirit of this book, and from the viewpoint of people who have criticized overreliance on statistical analyses, it is concepts, ideas, and hypotheses about what goes on in the world that are crucial.

Ultimately, the relevance of statistics to the work reported in this book must be decided by the intended use of the work. This book is not written to prove anything; proof does not even seem possible. My intent is to persuade people that certain ways of thinking about grief are plausible, at least in the case of some griefs. In the social and psychological study of human beings, the pursuit of ultimate truth, of immutable facts with simple, incontrovertible interpretations, seems impossible. What can be offered are perspectives, guesses, and understandings. These may not fit all situations, so they may not necessarily be replacements for former perspectives, guesses, and understandings. But, like corrective lenses for a person who has not been seeing too well, they may help one find that there is more going on in the world than one supposed, or that what one supposed is there can be seen more clearly.

Statistical Analyses to Accompany Chapter 4: The Anticipation of Deaths and Separations

Table 4.1 shows correlations, for each of the three years following separation, between the number of days of anticipating loss and the proportion of diary entries with grief. The variation in number of cases in Table 4.1 is, of course, due to variation in available data. The correlations in the table are based on losses, not diarists, so some diarists contributed more than one piece of data to a given correlation. It can be seen in Table 4.1 that grief tends to be less for separations when there has been greater time for anticipation of the loss. Twenty-seven of the 28 correlations are negative. The case attrition is great

Table 4.1. Grief and the Anticipation of Separation (Correlation of Proportion of Entries Containing Grief with Number of Days of Anticipating Separation)

Month	Year 1		Year 2		Year 3	
	r	n	r	n	r	n
1	−.02	55	−.15	16	−	11
2	−.04	52	−.08	15	−.19	11
3	−.13	34	−.13	14	−.16	10
4	−.07	27	−	14	−.14	11
5	−.14	23	.60	13	−	10
6	−.14	23	−.12	14	−.17	10
7	−.08	21	−.04	13	−	9
8	−.05	17	−.14	13	−	7
9	−.15	16	−	13	−.20	9
10	−.16	15	−.14	11	−	9
11	−	16	−.10	10	−.21	9
12	−.10	16	−.13	9	−.15	11

r = product moment correlation; n = number of cases of separation.
− = no r because no variance on grief (no case had grief for that month).

for separation because many separations ended in reunion. The trend in the correlational data for separations is weak; the negative correlations are quite close to .00. But from the correlations one might suspect that anticipation of a separation can mute grief for the lost person.

Table 4.2 provides, for duration of anticipation and grief in the case of deaths, a concise overview of correlational data like those presented in Table 4.1. In the top row of numbers in Table 4.2 it can be seen that for all deaths there is no clear patterning to the relationship of anticipation of loss to grief. For each year following the loss roughly half the monthly correlations of proportion of entries containing grief for the lost with number of days anticipating the loss are positive and roughly half are negative. (For each month, of course, some cases would be excluded because there were no diary entries for that particular month; and for some months after the first year there is no variability on grief—no diary contains grief—so no correlation coefficient can be computed.) When the data are separated into cases in which the diarist was or was not living with the deceased, patterning emerges. For deaths of people with whom the diarist was living, the pattern of relationship of anticipation and grief seems unsystematic. These correlations are summarized in the second line of Table 4.2. However, as the third line of Table 4.2 indicates, when diarists were not living with the deceased, anticipation tended to be associated with less grief in the first two years of loss.

Table 4.2. Grief and the Anticipation of Death (Correlation of Proportion of Entries Containing Grief with Number of Days of Anticipating the Death

| | Proportion of Correlations That Are Negative | | | Mean Number of Cases for Correlation Coefficients |
	Year 1	Year 2	Year 3	
All deaths	7/12	5/10	6/10	73
Deaths: Diarist and deceased coresident	7/12	5/10	2/4	23
Deaths: Diarist and deceased not coresident	11/12	6/6	5/9	51

Statistical Analyses to Accompany Chapter 8

In Table 8.1 are summarized correlations between offspring age and monthly data on grief. As the text in Chapter 8 indicates, there is no clear relationship between offspring age and parental grief when parent and offspring were living together at the time of offspring death. For months in which at least one diarist was judged to have a diary entry with grief, in about half the months older offspring age is associated with a higher proportion of diary entries with grief, and for about half the months older offspring age is associated with a lower proportion of diary entries with grief.

For noncoresident offspring, as the lower line in Table 8.1 and as the text in Chapter 8 indicate, older offspring age is associated with a smaller proportion of diary entries indicating parental grief. When diarist and offspring were not living together, the older the offspring, the less was the grief at his or her death.

Table 8.1. Correlations between Offspring Age and Monthly Data on Grief

| | Proportion of Months with Positive Correlations between Offspring Age and Parental Grief | | |
	Year 1	Year 2	Year 3
Coresident offspring	6/11	2/3	1/2
Noncoresident offspring	1/10	0/3	0/8

Statistical Analysis to Accompany Chapter 9

In Table 9.2 are the correlations for the first two months of grief, for both separations and deaths, between number of previous recorded losses in the diary and the proportion of diary entries with grief. All correlations are negative, which means that in those first two months the diarists with more previous losses recorded grief in fewer entries. The mechanisms that may underlie this are discussed in Chapter 9.

Table 9.2. Correlation of Grief with Number of Losses Recorded Previously in Diary

| Month of Bereavement | Deaths | | Separations | |
	r	n	r	n
First	−.15	127	−.18	170
Second	−.15	115	−.14	155

Bibliography

Bibliography

Ahern, Emily M. *The Cult of the Dead in a Chinese Village*. Stanford, CA: Stanford University Press, 1976.

Ahlstrom, Sydney E. *A Religious History of the American People*. New Haven, CT: Yale University Press, 1972.

Aries, Philippe. The reversal of death: Changes in attitudes toward death in western societies. *American Quarterly*, 1974, *26*, 536-560.

Averill, James R. Grief: Its nature and significance. *Psychological Bulletin*, 1968, *70*, 721-748.

Bakan, David. The test of significance in psychological research. *Psychological Bulletin*, 1977, *66*, 423-437.

Ball, Justine F. Widow's grief: The impact of age and mode of death. *Omega*, 1977, 7, 307-333.

Basch, Norma. Invisible women: The legal fiction of marital unity in nineteenth century America. *Feminist Studies*, 1979, *5*, 346-366.

Becker, Ernest. *The Denial of Death*. New York: Free Press, 1973.

Berger, Peter L., & Kellner, Hansfried. Marriage and the construction of reality. *Diogenes*, 1964, *46*, 1-24.

Bertman, Sandra L. Lingering terminal illness and the family: Insights from literature. *Family Process*, 1980, *19*, 341-348.

Bluebond-Langner, Myra. *The Private Worlds of Dying Children*. Princeton: Princeton University Press, 1977.

Bornstein, Philipp E., Clayton, Paula J., Halikas, James A., Maurice, William L., & Robins, Eli. The depression of widowhood after thirteen months. *British Journal of Psychiatry*, 1973, *122*, 561-566.

Bower, Gordon H. Mood and memory. *American Psychologist*, 1981, *36*, 129-148.

Bowlby, John. Process of mourning. *International Journal of Psycho-Analysis*, 1961, *42*, 317-340.

Bowlby, John. *Attachment and Loss*, Vol. III, *Loss*. Basic Books, 1980.

Bowlby, John, & Parkes, C. Murray. Separation and loss within the family. In E. James

Anthony & Cyrille Koupernik (Eds.), *The Child in his Family*. New York: Wiley-Interscience, 1970, pp. 197-216.

Brissett, Dennis, & Edgley, Charles (Eds.). *Life as Theater*. Chicago: Aldine, 1975.

Bugen, Larry A. Human grief: A model for prediction and intervention. *American Journal of Orthopsychiatry*, 1977, 47, 196-206.

Burge, Dolly Lunt. *The Diary of Dolly Lunt Burge*. (J. T. Robertson, Jr., Ed.). Athens: University of Georgia Press, 1962.

Burgess, Ann Wolbert, & Lazare, Aaron. *Community Mental Health*. Englewood Cliffs, NJ: Prentice-Hall, 1976.

Carey, Raymond G. The widowed: A year later. *Journal of Counseling Psychology*, 1977, 24, 125-131.

Clayton, Paula J. The effect of living alone on bereavement symptoms. *American Journal of Psychiatry*, 1975, 132, 133-137.

Clayton, Paula J. Bereavement. In E. S. Paykel (Ed.) *Handbook of Affective Disorders*. Edinburgh: Churchill Livingston, 1982, pp. 403-415.

Clayton, Paula J., Desmarais, Lynn, & Winokur, George. A study of normal bereavement. *American Journal of Psychiatry*, 1968, 125, 168-178.

Cott, Nancy F. *The Bonds of Womanhood*. New Haven, CT: Yale University Press, 1977.

DeVaul, R. A., Zisook, Sidney, & Faschingbauer, Thomas R. Clinical aspects of grief and bereavement. *Primary Care*, 1979, 6, 391-402.

Donaldson, P. J. Denying death: A note regarding some ambiguities in the current discussion. *Omega*, 1972, 3, 285-290.

Douglas, Ann. Heaven our home: Consolation literature in the northern United States, 1830-1880. *American Quarterly*, 1974, 26, 496-515.

Douglas, Ann. *The Feminization of American Culture*. New York: Knopf, 1977.

Dumont, Richard G., & Foss, Dennis C. *The American View of Death: Acceptance or Denial?* Cambridge, MA: Schenkman, 1972.

Faragher, John Mack. *Women and Men on the Overland Trail*. New Haven, CT: Yale University Press, 1979.

Farrell, James J. *Inventing the American Way of Death*. Philadelphia: Temple University Press, 1980.

Fischhoff, Baruch. Hindsight ≠ foresight: The effect of outcome knowledge on judgment under uncertainty. *Journal of Experimental Psychology: Human Perception and Performance*, 1975, 1, 288-299.

Fischhoff, Baruch. Perceived informativeness of facts. *Journal of Experimental Psychology: Human Perception and Performance*, 1977, 3, 349-358.

Fischhoff, Baruch. For those condemned to study the past: Reflections on historical judgment. In R. A. Shweder & D. W. Fiske (Eds.), *New Directions for Methodology of Behavioral Science: Fallible Judgment in Behavioral Research*. San Francisco: Jossey-Bass, 1980.

Fothergill, Robert A. *Private Chronicles: A Study of English Diaries*. New York: Oxford University Press, 1974.

Freud, Sigmund. Mourning and melancholia. In *Collected Papers of Sigmund Freud*, Vol 4, *Papers on Metapsychology, Papers on Applied Psychoanalysis*. New York: Basic Books, 1959, pp. 152-170. (Originally published in 1917).

Fulton, Robert, & Gottesman, David J. Anticipatory grief: A psychosocial concept reconsidered. *British Journal of Psychiatry*, 1980, 137, 45-54.

Futterman, Edward H., Hoffman, Irwin, & Sabshin, Melvin. Parental anticipatory mourning. In B. Schoenberg, A. C. Carr, D. Peretz, and A. H. Kutscher (Eds.), *Psychosocial Aspects of Terminal Care*. New York: Columbia University Press, 1972, pp. 243-272.

Gage, M. Geraldine. Economic roles of wives and family economic development. *Journal of Marriage and the Family*, 1975, *37*, 121-128.

Gauthier, Janel, & Marshall, W. L. Grief: A cognitive-behavioral analysis. *Cognitive Therapy and Research*, 1977, *1*, 39-44.

Gerber, Irwin, Rusalem, Roslyn, Hannon, Natalie, Battin, Delia, & Arkin, Arthur. Anticipatory grief and aged widows and widowers. *Journal of Gerontology*, 1975, *30*, 225-229.

Glick, Ira O., Weiss, Robert S., & Parkes, C. Murray. *The First Year of Bereavement*. New York: Wiley, 1974.

Goin, Marcia K., Burgoyne, R. W., & Goin, John M. Timeless attachment to a dead relative. *American Journal of Psychiatry*, 1979, *136*, 988-989.

Goode, William J. *Women in Divorce*. New York: Free Press, 1965.

Gorer, Geoffrey. *Death, Grief, and Mourning*. Garden City, NY: Doubleday Anchor, 1967.

Grabill, Wilson H., Kiser, Clyde V., & Whelpton, Pascal K. *The Fertility of American Women*. New York: Wiley, 1958.

Grigg, Susan. Toward a theory of remarriage: A case study in Newburyport at the beginning of the nineteenth century. *Journal of Interdisciplinary History*, 1977, *8*, 183-220.

Gut, Emmy. Some aspects of adult mourning. *Omega*, 1974, *5*, 323-342.

Habenstein, Robert W., & Lamers, William M. *The History of American Funeral Directing*. Milwaukee: Bulfin, 1962.

Heimlich, H. J., & Kutscher, A. H. The family's reaction to terminal illness. In B. Schoenberg, A. C. Carr, D. Peretz, & A. H. Kutscher (Eds.), *Loss and Grief: Psychological Management in Medical Practice*. New York: Columbia University Press, 1970, pp. 270-279.

Hempstead, Stephen. I at home. (D. O. Jensen, Ed.), *Missouri Historical Society Bulletin*. 1956, *13*, 30-56; 1957, *13*, 283-317; 1957, *14*, 59-96; 1958, *14*, 272-288; 1958, *15*, 38-48; 1959, *15*, 224-247; 1965, *22*, 61-94; 1966, *22*, 180-206, 410-445.

Hill, Charles, Rubin, Zick, & Peplau, Letitia A. Breakups before marriage: The end of 103 affairs. *Journal of Social Issues*, 1976, *32*, 147-168.

Hill, Reuben, & Rodgers, Roy H. The Developmental approach. In H. T. Christensen (Ed.), *Handbook of Marriage and the Family*. Chicago: Rand McNally, 1964, 171-211.

Hobson, C. J. Widows at Blackton. *New Society*, 1964, 24 September 13-16.

Ilick, Joseph E. Child-rearing in seventeenth century England and America. In L. deMause (Ed.), *The History of Childhood*. New York: Psychohistory Press, 1977, pp. 303-350.

Isen, Alice M., Shalker, Thomas E., Clark, Margaret, & Karp, Lynn. Affect accessibility of material in memory, and behavior: A cognitive loop? *Journal of Personality and Social Psychology*, 1978, *36*, 1-12.

Jensen, G. D., & Wallace, J. G. Family mourning process. *Family Process*, 1967, *6*, 56-66.

Johnson, Patricia A., & Rosenblatt, Paul C. Grief following childhood loss of parent. *American Journal of Psychotherapy*, 1981, *35*, 419-425.

Kendall, Philip C., & Hollon, Steven D. (Eds.). *Cognitive Behavioral Interventions*. New York: Academic Press, 1979.

Keyser, Linka. *Linka's Diary*. (J. C. K. Preus & D. M. Preus, Translators & Eds.), Minneapolis: Augsburg, 1952.

Kintsch, Walter. *Learning, Memory and Conceptual Processes*. New York: Wiley, 1970.

Koren, Elisabeth. *The Diary of Elisabeth Koren*. (D. T. Nelson, Translator & Ed.), Northfield, MN: Norwegian-American Historical Association, 1955.

Koriat, Asher, Melkman, Rachel, Averill, James R., & Lazarus, Richard S. The self-control of emotional reactions to a stressful film. *Journal of Personality*, 1972, *40*, 601-619.

Krell, Robert, & Rabkin, Leslie. The effects of sibling death on the surviving child: A family perspective. *Family Process*, 1979, *18*, 471-477.

Krupp, G. R., & Kligfeld, B. The bereavement reaction: A cross-cultural evaluation. *Journal of Religion and Health*, 1962, *1*, 222-246.

Kubler-Ross, E. *On Death and Dying*. New York: Macmillan, 1969.

Kuhn, Thomas S. *The Structure of Scientific Revolutions*. Chicago, IL: University of Chicago Press, 1962.

Lanzetta, John T., Cartwright-Smith, Jeffrey, & Kleck, Robert E. Effects of nonverbal dissimulation on emotional experience and autonomic arousal. *Journal of Personality and Social Psychology*, 1976, *33*, 354-370.

Lazarus, Richard S. The self-regulation of emotion. In L. Levi (Ed.), *Emotions: Their Parameters and Measurement*. New York: Raven Press, 1975.

Lederer, William J., & Jackson, Don D. *The Mirages of Marriage*. New York: Norton, 1968.

Lerner, Jeffrey. *The Public and Private Management of Death in Britain, 1890-1930*. Unpublished doctoral dissertation, Columbia University, 1981.

Lewis, C. S. *A Grief Observed*. New York: Seabury, 1961.

Lindemann, Erich. Symptomatology and management of acute grief. *American Journal of Psychiatry*, 1944, *101*, 141-148.

Lopata, Helena Z. *Widowhood in an American City*. Cambridge, MA: Schenkman, 1973.

Lopata, Helena Z. On widowhood: Grief work and identity reconstruction. *Journal of Geriatric Psychiatry*, 1975, *8*, 41-55.

Lopata, Helena Z. Widowhood and husband sanctification. *Journal of Marriage and the Family*, 1981, *43*, 439-450.

Lykken, David T. Statistical significance in psychological research. *Psychological Bulletin*, 1968, *70*, 151-159.

Maddison, David, & Walker, Wendy L. Factors affecting the outcome of conjugal bereavement. *British Journal of Psychiatry*, 1967, *113*, 1057-1067.

Mahoney, Michael J., & Thoresen, Carl E. *Self-Control: Power to the Person*. Monterey, CA: Brooks/Cole, 1974.

Mallory, Mary Alice Shutes. *Diary of Mary Alice Mallory*. Bloomington, IL: L. L. Shutes, 1967.

Marris, Peter. *Widows and Their Families*. London: Routledge & Kegan Paul, 1958.

Marris, Peter. *Loss and Change*. New York: Pantheon, 1974.

Matchett, William Foster. Repeated hallucinatory experiences as part of the mourning process among Hopi Indian women. *Psychiatry*, 1972, *35*, 185-194.

Matthews, William. *Canadian Diaries and Autobiographies*. Berkeley & Los Angeles: University of California Press, 1950.

Matthews, William. *American Diaries: An Annotated Bibliography of American Diaries Written Prior to the Year 1861*. Boston: Canner, 1959.

Matthews, William. *American Diaries in Manuscript, 1580-1954: A Descriptive Bibliography*. Athens: University of Georgia Press, 1974.

Meichenbaum, Donald, & Goodman, Sherryl. Clinical use of private speech and critical questions about its study of natural settings. In G. Zivin (Ed.), *The Development of Self-Regulation Through Private Speech*. New York: Wiley, 1979, pp. 325-360.

Mischel, Walter. On the interface of cognition and personality: Beyond the person-situation debate. *American Psychologist*, 1979, *34*, 740-754.

Mischel, Walter, & Patterson, Charlotte J. Substantive and structural elements of effective plans for self-control. *Journal of Personality and Social Psychology*, 1976, *34*, 942-950.

Moore, R. Laurence. The spiritualist medium: A study of female professionalism in Victorian America. *American Quarterly*, 1975, *27*, 200-221.

Nelson, Geoffrey K. *Spiritualism and Society*. London: Routledge & Kegan Pual, 1969.

Nevaldine, Anne. *Divorce: The Leaver and the Left*. Unpublished doctoral dissertation, University of Minnesota, 1978.

Parkes, C. Murray. The first year of bereavement: A longitudinal study of the reactions of London widows to the death of their husbands. *Psychiatry*, 1970, *33*, 444-467.

Parkes, C. Murray. *Bereavement: Studies of Grief in Adult Life*. New York: International Universities Press, 1972.

Parkes, C. Murray. Unexpected and untimely bereavement: A statistical study of young Boston widows and widowers. In B. Schoenberg, I. Gerber, A. Wiener, A. H. Kutscher, D. Peretz, & A. C. Carr (Eds.), *Bereavement: Its Psychosocial Aspects*. New York: Columbia University Press, 1975a.

Parkes, C. Murray. Determinants of outcome following bereavement. *Omega*, 1975b, *6*, 303-323.

Parkes, C. Murray. The emotional impact of cancer of ear, nose, and throat on patients and their families. *Journal of Laryngology and Otology*, 1975c, *89*, 1271-1279.

Parkes, C. Murray. Anticipatory grief (letter). *British Journal of Psychiatry*, 1981, *138*, 183.

Paul, Norman L., & Grosser, George H. Operational mourning and its role in conjoint family therapy. *Community Mental Health Journal*, 1965, *1*, 339-345.

Peppers, Larry G., & Knapp, Ronald J. *Motherhood and Mourning: Perinatal Death*. New York: Praeger, 1980.

Phillips, Martin W. Diary of a Mississippi Planter, January 1, 1840, to April, 1863. (F. L. Riley, Ed.), *Publications of the Mississippi Historical Society*, 1909, *10*, 305-481.

Pine, Vanderlyn R. Dying, death, and social behavior. In B. Schoenberg et al. (Eds.) *Anticipatory Grief*. New York: Columbia University Press, 1974, pp. 31-47.

Pollock, George H. Mourning and adaptation. *International Journal of Psycho-Analysis*, 1961, *42*, 341-361.

Rees, W. D. The hallucinations of widowhood. *British Medical Journal*, 1971, *4*, 37-41.

Ricouer, Paul. *Freud and Philosophy*. D. Savage (Translator), New Haven: Yale University Press, 1970.

Rosenblatt, Paul C. Ethnographic case studies. In M. Brewer & B. Collins (Eds.), *Scientific Inquiry and the Social Sciences*. San Francisco: Jossey-Bass, 1981, pp. 194-225.

Rosenblatt, Paul C., Peterson, P., Portner, J., Cleveland, M., Mykkanen, A., Foster, R., Holm, G., Joel, B., Reisch, H., Kreuscher, C., & Phillips, R. A cross-cultural study of responses to childlessness. *Behavioral Science Notes*, 1973, *8*, 221-231.

Rosenblatt, Paul C., & Titus, Sandra L. Together and apart in the family. *Humanitas*, 1976, *12*, 367-379.

Rosenblatt, Paul C., Walsh, R. Patricia, & Jackson, Douglas A. *Grief and Mourning in Cross-Cultural Perspective*. New Haven, CT: Human Relations Area Files Press, 1976.

Rosenblatt, Paul C., & Wright, Sara E. Shadow realities in close relationships. Unpublished manuscript.

Sanders, Catherine M. Comparison of younger and older spouses in bereavement outcome. *Omega*, 1980-1981, *11*, 217-232.

Sanford, Mollie Dorsey. *Mollie: The Journal of Mollie Dorsey Sanford in Nebraska and Colorado Territories, 1857-1866*. Lincoln: University of Nebraska Press, 1959.

Saum, Lewis O. Death in the popular mind of pre-Civil War America. *American Quarterly*, 1974, *26*, 477-495.

Scott, Anne Firor. *The Southern Lady*. Chicago: University of Chicago Press, 1970.

Silver, Roxane L., & Wortman, Camille B. Coping with undesirable life events. In J. Garber & M. E. P. Seligman (Eds.), *Human Helplessness*. New York: Academic Press, 1980, pp. 279-340.

Silverman, Phyllis R. Anticipatory grief from the perspective of widowhood. In B. Schoenberg et al. (Eds.) *Anticipatory Grief*. New York: Columbia University Press, 1974, pp. 320-330.

Silverman, S. M., & Silverman, Phyllis R. Parent-child communication in widowed families. *American Journal of Psychotherapy*, 1979, *33*, 428-441.

Sklar, Kathryn Kish. *Catherine Beecher: A Study in American Domesticity*. New Haven: Yale University Press, 1973.

Stannard, David E. Death and the Puritan child. *American Quarterly*, 1974, *26*, 456-476.

Stannard, David E. *The Puritan Way of Death*. New York: Oxford University Press, 1977.

Sunley, Robert. Early nineteenth-century American literature on child rearing. In M. Mead & M. Wolfenstein (Eds.), *Childhood in Contemporary Cultures*. Chicago: University of Chicago Press, 1955, pp. 150-167.

Titus, Sandra L., Rosenblatt, Paul C., & Anderson, Roxanne. Family conflict over inheritance of property. *Family Coordinator*, 1979, *28*, 337-346.

United States Bureau of the Census. *Historical Statistics of the United States: Colonial Times to 1970, Part 1*. Washington: U.S. Government Printing Office, 1975.

van Gennep, Arnold. *The Rites of Passage*. M. B. Vizedom & G. L. Caffee (Translators), Chicago: University of Chicago Press, 1960.

Vinovskis, Maris A. Angels' heads and weeping willows: Death in early America. *Proceedings of the American Antiquarian Society*, 1976, *86* (Part 2), 273-302.

Walker, Elkanah. *Nine Years with the Spokane Indians: The Diary of Elkanah Walker, 1838-1848*. (C. M. Drury, Ed.), Glendale, CA: Arthur H. Clark, 1976.

Walker, Mary Richardson (Mrs. Elkanah Walker). *First White Women Over the Rockies*, Vol. II. (C. M. Drury, Ed.), Glendale, CA: Arthur H. Clark, 1963.

Waller, Willard. *The Old Love and the New*. Carbondale, IL: Southern Illinois University Press, 1967. Originally published by Liveright, 1930.

Ward, Lester. *Young Ward's Diary*. (B. J. Stern, Ed.), New York: Putnam's, 1935.

Weiss, Robert S. *Marital Separation*. New York: Basic Books, 1975.

Welter, Barbara. *Dimity Convictions: The American Woman in the Nineteenth Century*. Athens, OH: Ohio University Press, 1976.

Wertheim, Eleanor S. Family unit therapy and the science and typology of family systems. *Family Process*, 1973, *12*, 361-376.

Winch, Robert F., & Campbell, Donald T. Proof? No! Evidence? Yes! *American Sociologist*, 1969, *4*, 140-143.

Woodward, Mary Dodge. *The Checkered Years*. (M. B. Cowdrey, Ed.), Caldwell, ID: Caxton, 1937.

Wretmark, G. A. study in grief reactions. *Acta Psychiatrica et Neurologica Scandinavica*, Supplement 136, 1959, *34*, 292-299.

Wrigley, E. A. Family limitation in pre-industrial England. In O. Ranum & P. Ranum (Eds.), *Popular Attitudes Toward Birth Control in Pre-Industrial France and England*. New York: Harper & Row, 1972, pp. 53-99.

Yamamoto, Joe, Okonogi, Keigo, Iwasaki, Tetsuga, & Yoshimura, Saburo. Mourning in Japan. *American Journal of Psychiatry*, 1969, *125*, 1660-1665.

Indexes

Subject Index

Anniversaries, 15, 25, 27-28, 31, 34, 63, 94, 133, 154, 155
Autopsy, 26, 67, 68

Bible, 44, 66, 73, 108, 138
Birth control, 56-57
Birthdays, 25, 26, 154
Burial, 26, 27, 42, 66, 67, 93, 125, 128, 134, 149

Canada, 3, 9, 10, 16, 18-19, 24, 27, 57, 63, 64, 65, 66-67, 72-73, 94, 126, 119-30, 133, 143, 169, 175, 176, 177, 178, 179
Child labor, 55
Christmas, 25, 154
Civil War, 12, 14, 18, 49, 56, 65, 72-73
Consolation literature, 15
Coresidence, 37, 50-51, 52, 82-84, 89-90, 91-92, 93, 95-98, 111, 135, 157-58, 160-61, 183, 184
Crying, 27, 35, 41, 44, 49, 57, 72, 73, 74, 85, 109, 113, 128, 129, 133, 145, 146

Death(s): in childbirth, 17, 57, 59, 61-65, 66-67, 70, 159, 184; fear of, 22, 62-63, 65, 70, 118; of grandchild, 41; of grandparent, 66, 90; of infant or young child, 12, 17, 18, 23, 24, 41-42, 53-61, 67, 89, 90, 91-93, 96, 102, 103, 106-07, 117, 128, 145, 149, 159, 169, 184; of mature offspring, 37, 63, 64, 65, 66, 84, 90, 91-93, 113-14, 115, 117, 128-32, 148, 169; number of, in sample, 13; of parent, 17, 18, 27, 62, 66, 69, 72, 89, 90, 93-94, 106, 114, 121, 129, 131, 133, 138-39, 140-43, 144, 146, 147, 169; of pet, 13, 124-25, 126, 179; seasonal pattern, 54-55; of sibling, 34, 44, 49, 62, 63, 72-73, 89, 90-91, 107, 108, 149; of spouse, 17, 21, 22-23, 27, 42, 43, 58-60, 62, 63-64, 66, 69, 74, 89, 94-95, 96, 98, 102, 106, 108, 110, 115-16, 117, 126, 133-34, 137, 138, 139-40, 143, 145-47, 155, 169; violent, 11; watch, 26, 66, 67; wish, 35. *See also* Grief
Delayed realization of loss, 18-19
Denial, 18-19, 122-23, 155
Depression, 3, 25, 31, 32, 35, 111, 121, 147, 148
Diaries: advantages and disadvantages of, as research material, 5-7, 10, 11-13, 17-18, 23, 24, 36, 43, 46, 51, 69, 117, 118, 135, 161-62, 169-73; bibliographic aids to study of, 10; ethics of studying, 8, 165-69; first entries of loss in, 16-19, 25, 119-20, 133, 152; privacy, 169-73; published vs. unpublished, 10, 11; role in emotional control, 110; role in grief work, 40, 117, 119; sample, 7-14; validity of use in understanding grief, 16-31, 118-19. *See also* specific diaries listed in Appendix B
Divorce, 16, 81, 98

195

Name Index

Paul C. Rosenblatt earned his doctorate in psychology at Northwestern University in 1962. He has taught at the University of Missouri, Columbia, the University of California, Riverside, and, since 1969, at the University of Minnesota, where he is a professor in the department of family social science. He is co-author (with R. Patricia Walsh and Douglas A. Jackson) of *Grief and Mourning in Cross-Cultural Perspective* and has written many articles on marital and familial relations.